The
Holy
Trinity

THE
HOLY
TRINITY

Experience and Interpretation

by GEORGE HEDLEY

FORTRESS PRESS   PHILADELPHIA

© 1967 by Fortress Press

Library of Congress Catalog Card Number LC-67-16468

3675A67   Printed in U.S.A.   1-96

GLORY BE TO THE FATHER, AND TO THE SON, AND TO THE HOLY GHOST; AS IT WAS IN THE BEGINNING, IS NOW, AND EVER SHALL BE, WORLD WITHOUT END. AMEN.

Contents

	Page
Introduction: THE CHALLENGES	ix
THE BACKGROUNDS	1
I. Plurality to Unity	1
II. The Spirit of the Lord	10
III. Sons of God	20
THE EXPERIENCE	27
IV. The Lord Incarnate	28
V. The Lord in Residence	40
VI. The Lord Eternal	50
THE FORMULATION	63
VII. The Road to Nicea	63
VIII. Disputings and Definings	83
IX. *In Essentia Unitas*	103
Continuance: THE REALITIES	119
NOTES	131
INDEX	145

The Challenges

IN 1963 Bishop John A. T. Robinson of Woolwich, honestly seeking to be *Honest to God*,[1] urged that Christians of today ought to abandon much of the phrasing which historically has been used to convey Christian thought. In 1964 Bishop James A. Pike of California dismissed the doctrine of the Holy Trinity as an old bottle which, in *A Time for Christian Candor*,[2] inevitably is going to burst, and whose bursting should occasion no regrets. Six years before that, though securing much less of public notice, Professor Cyril C. Richardson of Union Theological Seminary had concluded and declared that *The Doctrine of the Trinity* "is an artificial construct. . . . It produces confusion rather than clarification. . . . There is no necessary threeness in the Godhead." [3]

In our day the problem of the Trinity as such may seem to have been bypassed altogether by the announcement of *The Death of God*.[4] If there be no God, then any attempt to analyze his being is obviously meaningless. Not only the specific affirmations of Christian faith, but any kind of affirmation about God at all, would be overridden by the one sweeping negation.

Undeniably it is difficult in our time to maintain faith

in a living God. It must be remembered, however, that such a faith never has been easy to hold. Faith has been challenged always, even as it is now, both by natural evil in our world and by moral evil in our society. Faith has been rejected time and again by the ignorant and the indifferent, and also by many of the learned and the thoughtful. Faith yet has persisted. In its persistence it ever has demanded not only acceptance, but also an attempt at understanding.

One such attempt, one attempt albeit a very complex and slowly developing one, was the formulation of the Christian doctrine of the Holy Trinity. It is not to be denied that this doctrine has produced confusion, and that it still does. It is true that the word "Trinity" is not to be found in the Holy Scriptures, nor in the Apostles' nor the Nicene Creed. A teaching which seems thus not to stem from original Christianity, and which appears not to be understood in our time, naturally enough is suspect both from the standpoint of modernity and from that of antiquity.

It is tempting, and it is easy, to ignore the unfamiliar and to discard the puzzling. Nevertheless it is dangerous to ignore what we have not examined, and it is dishonest to deny what we have not tried to understand. Before we assent to the dismissal of any historic Christian teaching, we owe it to ourselves and to the Christian community to enquire into that teaching's origins, its intent, its history, and its possible services to those who have assented to it.

How did this particular doctrine of the Holy Trinity come into being? What assumptions, in the minds of its formulators, lay behind it? What experiences in their lives did it reflect? What meanings was it intended to convey to Christian believers? What values of Christian faith and life was it designed to embody?

This little book will seek to identify the beginnings, and to trace something of the development, of Christian Trinitarian teaching. On these bases it will enquire into the significance of the teaching for the Church both ancient and modern.

Much of the discussion of the Trinity throughout the centuries has been argumentative, and not a little of it polemic. The present approach, however, will be more largely reportorial than editorial. So far as possible the great teachers of the Church will be trusted to speak for themselves, in their own several terms. They are not always easy to understand; but they are scarcely less clear than most of the commentators upon their works. The thoughtfully enquiring reader will profit by doing his own judging of the materials, with a minimum of modern scribal interposition.

Doctrine is always, and necessarily, an attempt to express ultimate truth within immediate words. Usually, and of necessity, doctrine but reflects rather than expresses. The question before us is whether the doctrine of the Holy Trinity may have worth, either as an expression of truth or as a reflection of truth, in our thinking today.

The
Backgrounds

NO SYSTEM of teaching, no specific doctrine, no single idea, ever has sprung suddenly into being out of nothing. These three opening chapters will attempt to identify some of the pre-Christian soil, some of the seeds, and some of the fertilizing agents, which made it possible for the Christian doctrine of the Holy Trinity to germinate, to take root, and to grow.

The soil, the seeds, and the nutrients were both Jewish and Gentile. So also the doctrine in its developed forms is both Gentile and Jewish. Father, Son, and Holy Spirit all are to be identified, in varying ways and to varying degrees, in the traditions both of Athens and of Jerusalem. The details of these identifications will engage our attention now.

I. PLURALITY TO UNITY

"Hear, O Israel: the Lord our God is one Lord." [1] Regular Jewish usage in English has phrased this as, "Hear, O Israel: The Lord our God, the Lord is One." [2] We Christians have regarded it as an unmistakable and emphatic statement of monotheism, and so for many centuries have the Jews. From this it has been inferred both that monotheism was the original faith of the Hebrew people, and that it was originally a Jewish contribution to the thought of the world. The realities are not nearly so simple.

The new Jewish version of the *Torah*[3] renders the *Shema Yisrael* in the form, "Hear, O Israel, the Lord is our God, the Lord alone." One vital point of understanding is suggested in this. It is "our God," the God of Israel, who is the subject: the God of Israel, not necessarily of the rest of mankind. Another important consideration remains obscured, for reasons of a tradition which we must now examine.

The Hebrew word represented by "Lord" in all of these translations is not at all the inclusive, generic term it seems to be in English. It is rather an identifying, particularizing proper name. Its consonants, which are equivalent to our *JHVH,* do appear in Hebrew Bibles; but its own vowels, possibly though not certainly ā and ĕ (thus "Jahveh") have yielded to those (ă, ō, and ā) which belong to the word *Adonai,* a term which actually does mean "Lord."

The only English version which attempts to make clear the character of *JHVH* as a proper name, the American Standard edition of 1901, does so in philological absurdity. Its "Jehovah" is but a clumsy reproducing of the Hebrew miscegenation of the *JHVH* consonants and the vowels of *Adonai.*

That miscegenation itself reflects what became, and has remained, the standard Jewish interpreting of the commandment, "Thou shalt not take the name of the Lord (*JHVH*) thy God in vain."[4] At least as early as New Testament times this had been intensified to mean, "Thou shalt not pronounce the divine name at all." In oral usage, therefore, *Adonai* ("Lord') was substituted for the forbidden *JHVH*. When six or more centuries later vowel markings were added to the consonantal Hebrew text, this customary substitution was indicated by the writing (though never the pronouncing) of the two words in the combined form we have noted.

The appearance of "the Lord" instead of "Jahveh" in our English translations thus is the written equivalent of the centuries-old oral practice of Judaism. The effect of both these usages has been to obscure much of the actual meaning of some familiar Old Testament passages. In the earlier (possibly eighth-century B.C.) of our two accounts of Moses' experience at the burning bush,[5] the young expatriate Israelite says that he does not know the name of the divine being who is speaking to him. The teller of the tale, after suggesting an etymology (a rather dubious one) in the Hebrew verb "to be" (*HYH*), goes on to identify not "the Lord God of your fathers" in our sense, but rather and very specifically, *"JHVH, God of your fathers."*

A much later treatment of the same episode denies that even the fathers had known the sacred name.[6] Yet in one of the earlier narratives it is said that men began to use the name as early as the time of Enos, the first grandson of Adam and Eve.[7] Here our united Jewish and Christian usage is particularly deceptive. The Genesis line should be read not "then began men to call upon the name of the Lord," but "then began men to say the name *JHVH*." What is critically important for us to recognize is that

3

this is an individualizing name with which we are dealing, and not by any means a universalizing title.

This name was the individual name of a God associated with a confederation of tribes which, long before the first writing down of any of its traditions, was well on the way toward becoming a nation. Already much progress had been made from the days when not just whole nations but small localities—even springs, trees, and winds—had been conceived as having their respective supernatural guardians, if not as being supernatural entities in themselves. There may be traces of this in the burning bush episode, and also in the several glimpses we get of *JHVH* as the thunder god of Mount Sinai.[8]

Rendered in the familiar forms of "the Lord our God is one Lord," and "The Lord our God, the Lord is one," our key statement suggests the very real possibility that popular religious thought at that time may have been acknowledging many more than one *JHVH*. The fact that the declaration stands in Deuteronomy tends to associate it with that book's primary concern, the effort to break down religious localism and to establish the Jerusalem temple as the only proper place for sacrificial worship. The Canaanite religion recognized many local *Baalim*. On this analogy there may have been a disposition for the Israelites to disintegrate and to localize *JHVH* as well.

The evident faith expressed in our passage, as possibly its intended and direct appeal, is in and for *JHVH* as the unitary God of Israel. The faith and the appeal, however, seem both to relate to *JHVH* as the God of Israel only. The injunction is precisely, "Hear, O Israel," and the dec-

4

laration relates specifically to "*JHVH* our God." There is no hint that *JHVH* is the God of other peoples of the period, let alone of the entire creation. If he were even international, let alone cosmic, he would require no individual name for his identifying. Despite the assured and unquestioning monotheism of the later Old Testament writers and editors, traces of the earlier and more limited pattern of thought survive at many points in the Hebrew Scriptures.

Thus "I am the Lord (*JHVH*) your God: fear not the gods of the Amorites, in whose land ye dwell" does not deny that the Amorite deities exist. It but says, with normal nationalistic pride, that *JHVH* is stronger than they are. ("My God can lick your god.") In the case of the capture of the Israelite ark of the covenant by the Philistines, and its installation as a prize of war in the temple of the Philistine god Dagon, it is not just an image, but the god himself, who is "fallen upon his face to the earth before the ark of the Lord" (*JHVH* again).[9]

Similarly we find that the Baalim of the Canaanites, and such deities as Chemosh of Moab and Molech (or Milcom) of Ammon, are assumed to be actual even if inferior beings. It is not nearly so much theological heresy as it is lack of patriotism which the narrator is condemning when he says that

> the children of Israel did evil in the sight of the Lord, and served Baalim: and they forsook the Lord God of their fathers, which brought them out of the land of Egypt, and followed other gods, of the gods of the people that were round about them.

In a speech ascribed to the Israelite "judge" Jephthah, the respective territorial domains of the deities are recognized as a matter of course:

> Wilt not thou possess that which Chemosh thy god giveth thee to possess? So whomsoever the Lord our God shall drive out from before us, them will we possess.

Certainly the great king Solomon was no monotheist, for we are told that he

> went after Astoreth the goddess of the Zidonians, and after Milcom the abomination of the Ammonites. . . . Then did Solomon build an high place for Chemosh, the abomination of Moab, in the hill that is before Jerusalem, and for Molech, the abomination of the children of Ammon.[10]

It is possible, of course, but by no means demonstrable, that the narrator in this last case has "demythologized" his materials in his own thinking. However that may be, what he reports of the king's thinking and practice points unmistakably to an accepted polytheism in the royal court. Further, what is evident in his treatment is that he disapproves of this primarily on grounds of disloyalty, in the monarch's not going "fully after the Lord (*JHVH*) as did David his father." [11]

Gradually, and almost imperceptibly from our so much later point of view, the national protector of Israel and the storm god of Sinai became coalesced as the one maker and ruler of heaven and earth. An early Semitic analogue of this unification may be seen in the person of Marduk, the city god of Babylon. Marduk, who appears as "Merodach" in the Hebrew,[12] is not only a municipal deity. He is at the same time the hero of the Babylonian creation myth, which antedates the earliest of the Hebrew writings by at least several centuries.

Direct Babylonian influence, however, is chiefly to be discerned in the later of the two Genesis narratives of the creation of the world.[13] This is part of the so-called "priestly document," in modern scholastic abbreviation "P," of approximately 450 B.C. P's account of the first things does not use the personal name *JHVH* at all. One god of the universe now is taken for granted, and therefore is sufficiently designated by the generic Hebrew term *Elohim,* "God."

Quite otherwise the more primitive narrative,[14] of some four hundred years earlier, sees its creative being as limited in three different ways. It identifies him specifically as the Israelite *JHVH.* It assigns his activity not to "the heavens and the earth," but only to the first making, on an earth already given, of man, plants, and animals (and of woman last of all). Finally, it regards this creator as physically and spatially conditioned, and curiously restricted both in his access to information and in his responses to events.

Perhaps at just about the chronological midpoint between these two Hebrew experiments in cosmogony, there appears a moral if not certainly a metaphysical monotheism in the preaching of the eighth-century prophet Amos. Without explicitly denying the existence of the gods of the other nations, the book of Amos manages effectively to ignore them. *JHVH,* it declares, "will roar from Zion, and utter his voice from Jerusalem"; but his activity is by no means limited to his own Hebrew terrain. He "will not turn away the punishment" of Syria to the northward, of

Philistia on the southwest border, of easterly Ammon and Moab.[15]

Though Amos is much less a theologian than he is a social evangelist, his moral passion carries him far into theological innovation. Not only does *JHVH* exercise power in and over alien lands. He is also quite free from any national chauvinism of his own. The prophet's whole attack on the misbehavior of the neighbors is but a deliberately disarming prelude to, and a foundation for, his flaming assault upon the sins of Israel: "For three transgressions of Israel, and for four, I will not turn away the punishment thereof." [16] This God, then, is not at all an uncritical defender of a nation to which he is specially and irrevocably committed. Objective and detached in his judgments, even if still somewhat excitable in his moods, he has moved far toward being a universal ruler.

A much gentler note is sounded, possibly though not assuredly soon after Amos' day, in the book of Hosea as now we know it. Whether or not this work really records the prophet's forgiving love for his errant wife, as in the popular romantic interpretation of its first three chapters, certainly in its present form it includes tenderness among the divine attributes as well as anger. It shows mercy accompanying justice and perhaps supplanting it.

> How shall I give thee up, Ephraim? how shall I deliver thee, Israel? . . . I will not execute the fierceness of mine anger, I will not return to destroy Ephraim: for I am God, and not man. . . . I will heal their backsliding: I will love them freely: for mine anger is turned away from him.[17]

It may be that this concept of a sensitive and humane *JHVH* developed after the Babylonian exile of the sixth century rather than before it, and that it was inserted into the book of Hosea as a counterweight to the devastating condemnations which unquestionably are native to the eighth century. In any case the assurance of the divine love became, and remained, a vital element in both the faith and the theology of Judaism.

JHVH has become the ruler of the universe, and emphatically so, in that section of the book of Isaiah (chapters 40-55) which was written during the exile itself. Here the God of the Jews is the sole determiner and director of world history. He calls Cyrus of Persia "his anointed" (*Mashiach* = "Messiah"). "I am *JHVH*," he says to this (presumably Zoroastrian) emperor,

> and there is none else, there is no God beside me: I girded thee, though thou hast not known me: that they may know from the rising of the sun, and from the west, that there is none beside me.

So absolute now is this monotheism that it leads its exponent into what many believers would consider to be an absurd and even immoral extreme: "I am *JHVH,* and there is none else. I form the light, and create darkness: I make peace, and create evil: I *JHVH* do all these things." [18]

Various attempts later were made to reconcile the omnipotence of a good God with the manifest existence of evil in the world. If here the prophet was reacting directly to Zoroastrian dualism, he would seem to be assigning to his one God the functions both of the good

Ormuzd and of the destructive Ahriman. It may be argued, however, that it is only natural calamity and not moral sinfulness which here is contrasted with "peace." If this be true, it becomes the easier to understand the rise of the concept of "the Satan" as we find it in later Old Testament writings and in the early Christian ones.[19]

In any event the conviction of the Lord's oneness, and the assurance that the God of Israel indeed was the "King of the universe," by now had become cardinal to Jewish faith. For Judaism after the exile, *"JHVH our God is one JHVH"* had moved far beyond any protest against regional and local disintegrations of a national deity, and far past insistence upon that deity's own national affiliation. It had become the climactic assertion of the character of *JHVH* as one and indivisible, the single Lord of Israel and of all mankind, the unitary ruler of the earth and of all creation.

II. THE SPIRIT OF THE LORD

Not long ago the present writer was working out a baccalaureate sermon to be called "The Time Ghost." A preliminarily scribbled outline noted the prevailing moods of recent decades, the spirits of their respective times, as "The Stuffy Ghost" before World War I; "The Romantic Ghost" of that wartime; "The Negative Ghost" of the postwar disillusion; and "The Frightened Ghost" of our own days. Shown that much of the proposed structure, scribbled in a notebook, a young Jewish lady remarked immediately, "Of course your conclusion will be that we need the Holy Ghost."

There is, or at least there should be, nothing surprising about such a discerning response on the part of a literate member of the Jewish community. "The Holy Ghost" is none other than the Divine Spirit; in the terminology of the Old Testament, "the Spirit of the Lord" or "the Spirit of God." The variations between "Lord" (*JHVH*) and "God" (*Elohim*) follow very largely the distinctions between early and late materials we noted in the preceding chapter. The concept of the Divine Spirit does not necessarily vary with these respective usages.

The most primitive of the Biblical materials treat God himself as an actor physically present on the earthly scene, and participating in human episodes. Thus he walks in the garden of Eden "in the cool of the day" (wisely having avoided the noonday sun), and discovers that Adam and Eve have been up to mischief. Similarly he personally visits Abraham's encampment on the plains of Mamre, and there allows himself to be talked into taking a more generous attitude toward Sodom and Gomorrah than at first he had held.[1]

Naïveté such as this could not long endure. The physical presence of God disappears from the narratives even as the perception of his spiritual character is intensified and refined. The first substitution is quasi-physical, or at least visible: that of the "angels," defined as "messengers" both by the Hebrew *malakim* and as the Greek *angeloi*.

It is not *JHVH* himself, but "the angel of the Lord," who intervenes to save the young Isaac on Mount Moriah. God's angel is the guide and guardian of the Israelites in their journeyings through the desert. Presumably it is this

11

same angel who scolds "all the children" of Israel for making entangling alliances with Canaanite tribes. Nevertheless he gives helpful (and very specific) instructions to Gideon, and he pays a most friendly visit to the couple who will become the parents of the heroic Samson.[2]

The two concepts are interestingly conjoined in what has reached us as an extremely mixed narrative about the young Jacob's night at Bethel. Here an eighth-century narrator (the one commonly called "E") portrays the traveler as seeing "the angels of God ascending and descending" on the ladder to heaven. Then, however, there is a swing back to a ninth-century version (J), which represents the Lord himself as delivering his own message.[3]

The next and enduring stage, after the transition from the physical presence of God to the mediation of angels, was the thought of the divine spirit, the *ruach Elohim.* The Hebrew word *ruach,* like the Greek *pneuma* and both *anima* and *spiritus* in the Latin, has at once physical and non-physical connotations. All four of these terms are used alike for "wind" and "breath," and also for what we would call "spiritual" entities. It is not always easy to determine which of these, or what sort of concept somewhere in between them, is intended in Old Testament usage.

Twenty-eight times in the King James version *ruach* is rendered by "breath." The physical aspect dominates in all of these, with the possible exception of the "breath" which comes from the Lord into Ezekiel's valley of dry bones. This sounds physical indeed. In the interpretation of the allegory which follows immediately after it, how-

12

ever, *ruach* is rendered necessarily as "spirit" in "shall put my spirit in you, and ye shall live." [4] The differentiation thus made in English does of course obscure the dual identity of the one word as it stands in the Hebrew.

A relatively late example of the physical emphasis appears in the later and more sophisticated of our two creation accounts, which says that "the Spirit of God moved [better, 'was moving'] upon the face of the waters." According well with this is the line in the (also late) book of Job, "By his spirit he hath garnished the heavens." Elsewhere in the same book, however, the 1611 version renders *ruach* physically even if symbolically: "by the breath of his nostrils they are consumed." [5]

The warning that "my spirit shall not always strive with man" is associated with mankind's physical survival, but obviously its primary reference is to moral struggles between the divine and the human. The presence of God's spirit with the brilliant young Joseph is recognized even by a pagan Pharaoh, and it is revealed in the granting of special skills to the metalsmith Bezaleel. A striking summary is ascribed to the aging Moses: "Would God that all the Lord's people were prophets, and that the Lord would put his spirit upon them!" [6]

After the entry into Canaan the spirit of the Lord is found directing and empowering the chieftains of Israel: in succession Othniel, Gideon (who, as we have seen, received instructions also from "the angel of the Lord"), Jephthah, and Samson. [7] In the last of these cases, one must admit, the effect of the spiritual visitation seems uniformly to have been one of physical violence.

At the time of the transition from tribal federation to a unified monarchy, the prophet Samuel promises the divine spirit to the new king Saul, and sees the pledge fulfilled almost immediately: "Is Saul also among the prophets?" Later the spirit of the Lord, having despaired of Saul and departed from him, "came upon David." "The last words of David . . . the sweet psalmist of Israel" begin, "The Spirit of the Lord spake by me, and his word was in my tongue." [8]

The earliest of the "writing prophets," Amos and Hosea, make no reference to the divine spirit, nor does Jeremiah, more than a century later. In most of the remainder of the prophetic books the spirit is regarded as causative, as much for revelation as for achievement. "The spirit of the Lord shall rest upon" the expected Messiah: spirit defined as that "of wisdom and understanding, the spirit of counsel and might, the spirit of knowledge and of the fear of the Lord." In the second major section of the book of Isaiah, the "suffering servant" of the Lord is likewise a bearer of the spirit. "I am full of power by the spirit of the Lord," declares the embattled farmer Micah, as he assails the tyrannies of metropolitan finance and the inequities of metropolitan justice.[9]

The spirit of the Lord grants to Ezekiel his own special visions, but that spirit will also be available to all "the house of Israel." In the book of Joel the promise is widened to provide for the outpouring of God's spirit "upon all flesh." It will not escape the reader's attention that the report of St. Peter's sermon after the descent of the Holy Spirit on the day of Pentecost, the first Whitsunday, includes the quoting of practically the entire paragraph from the prophecy of Joel.[10]

Two other prophetic passages, in particular, seem especially to point the way toward the later Christian acceptance and development of this authentically Jewish concept of "the spirit of God." One is the word of the late sixth-century Zechariah to the governor Zerubbabel, the first restorer of the ruined Jerusalem: "Not by might, nor by power, but by my spirit, saith the Lord of hosts." [11] This is the essence of the divine reality at work in the world, and immediately in the life of a man. Zechariah saw that reality in the rebuilding of the temple, and the apostles in the building of the Church.

A second definitive declaration is that which Jesus chose to quote when he read the Scriptures publicly in his home synagogue at Nazareth. It is from a probably late, though not certainly datable, addendum to the book of Isaiah:

> The Spirit of the Lord God is upon me; because the Lord hath anointed me to preach good tidings unto the meek: he hath sent me to bind up the brokenhearted, to proclaim liberty to the captives, and the opening of the prison to them that are bound; to proclaim the acceptable year of the Lord . . .[12]

That our Lord selected these lines to set forth his own view of his own experience and his own mission, immediately ties together the Christian revelation in Jesus the Christ and the Old Testament doctrine of the Spirit of God. Already, therefore, we find ourselves dealing with evident factors in the origins of the doctrine of the Holy Trinity.

After the close of the prophetic period, we find what may or may not be a cognate concept to that of the divine spirit, but which is certainly at some points a similar one, in the personified Wisdom of the book of Proverbs. "Doth not wisdom cry? and understanding put forth her voice?" Later in the same chapter we hear this Wisdom's voice declaring, "The Lord possessed me in the beginning of his way, before his works of old. I was set up from everlasting, from the beginning, or ever the earth was." Almost inevitably the Christian reader thinks here not only of the Spirit brooding over the waters at the creation, but also of the Fourth Gospel's divine Word which "was in the beginning with God." [13]

Later than the Proverbs, but earlier than the Gospel, is the apocryphal work called "The Wisdom of Solomon." Here Wisdom, by all means the leading character, is positively identified with the Spirit at the very outset: "For wisdom is a loving spirit. . . . For the Spirit of the Lord filleth the world: and that which containeth all things, hath knowledge of the voice." Again toward the end of the original text of this Hellenistic Jewish work, we find the question, "And thy counsel who hath known, except thou give wisdom, and send the Holy Spirit from above?" [14]

The great exemplar of Hellenistic Jewish thinking, Philo of Alexandria, seems to use the Hebrew *ruach* (Spirit) and *chokmah* (Wisdom) almost interchangeably, not only with each other but also with the Greek philosophers' *logos* (Word). "It is this Word," he says, "which one of Moses' company compared to a river, when he said in the Psalms 'the river of God which is full of water.' [15]

. . . He is representing the Divine Word as full of the stream of wisdom, with no part empty or devoid of itself." Philo speaks also, however, of "the divine spirit of wisdom." Of this he declares,

> One sort of men only does it aid with its presence, even those who, having disrobed themselves of all created things and of the innermost veil and wrapping of mere opinion, with mind unhampered and naked will come to God.[16]

Philo is fully aware of the difference between the physical and the metaphysical definitions of *ruach*:

> Now the name of the "spirit of God" is used in one sense for the air which flows up from the land, the third element which rides upon the water, and thus we find in the Creation-story "the spirit of God was moving over the water" . . . In another sense it is the pure knowledge in which every man naturally shares.[17]

As examples of the latter sense Philo cites the case of the inspiring of Bezaleel the metalsmith, which we have noted already, and also that of the sharing of "the spirit which is upon [Moses]" with a chosen company of seventy elders of Israel.[18] In this connection Philo says categorically that

> the spirit which is on him is the wise, the divine, the excellent spirit, susceptible of neither severance nor division, diffused in its fullness everywhere and through all things.[19]

We find, however, not only "Divine Spirit" (*theion pneuma*), but also and even more frequently "Divine Word" (*theios logos*). "Nothing mortal," we read,

> can be made in the likeness of the most high One and Father of the universe but (only) in that of the second God, who is His Logos. For it is right that the rational

(part) of the human soul should be formed as an impression by the divine Logos, since the pre-Logos God is
superior to every rational nature. . . . God most justly
avenges the virtuous and decent men because they have
a certain kinship with His Logos, of which the human
mind is a likeness and image.[20]

Thus also,

The world has come into being, and assuredly it has
done so under the hand of some Cause; and the Logos of
Him who makes it is Himself the Seal, by which each
thing that exists has received its shape. Accordingly from
the outset form in perfection accompanies the things that
come into being, for it is an impress and image of the
perfect Logos.[21]

It is interesting to speculate on what might have been
the effect on Christian theology, and especially on the
formulation of the doctrine of the Trinity, had Philo made
sharper distinctions among his three terms: Wisdom, Spirit,
and Word. It is at least conceivable that in this case both
the first and the fourteenth chapters of the Fourth Gospel
would have been differently written, and so that what we
know as the *logos* Christology would not have taken the
form in which we know it. The implications for the
filioque problem, that of the Spirit's proceeding from the
Father only or from both the Father and the Son,[22] are
fascinating too. That the Eastern and Western Churches
never have found agreement on this issue may be associated with the ambiguity in Philo's effort to correlate his
Greek with his Jewish concepts.

Much more definitely Hebraic, and correspondingly
much less abstruse, are the references to the divine Spirit
in the "Dead Sea Scrolls." "Only through the holy spirit,"

says the "Manual of Discipline," "can (one) achieve union with God's truth and be purged of all his iniquities." Every modern Jew, as well as every modern Christian, would feel at home with the benediction in the "Formulary of Blessings": "The Lord favor thee with the holy spirit, with lovingkindness." The "Book of Hymns" treats the Spirit as creative: "When first the world began Thou didst shed an holy spirit on all Thou didst bring into being"; but also as revelatory: "Through the Spirit Thou hast planted within me, I, Thy servant, am come to know that all Thy judgments are truth, and righteousness all Thy works, and ne'er shall Thy word be revoked"; and furthermore as sustaining: "I will give thanks unto Thee, O Lord, for by Thine own strength hast Thou stayed me, and hast wafted o'er me Thy holy spirit that I cannot be moved." "Thou didst shed thy holy spirit upon us," says an intercessory prayer of the Qumran brotherhood, "bringing to us thy blessings." [23]

There is, then, nothing about the concept of the Spirit of God which is alien to, or even uncommon in, the theological thinking and the religious experience of pre-Christian Judaism. Even as the Hebrew heritage contributed the faith in one God and Father of all, so also it made available to Christianity the identifying of that God as active on the earth, and among and within men and women, in the presence of the Holy Spirit. Greek thinking later entered into the pattern, as we shall see; but Greek thought was by no means essential to the basic doctrine. The Spirit of God, as the Jews were persuaded, had been moving upon the earthly scene from the first phases of the Creation onward.

III. SONS OF GOD

Some beings described as "sons of God" make a sudden and rather startling appearance in the Scriptures as early as the primitive "J" document in Genesis. "The sons of God," we read,

> saw the daughters of men that they were fair; and they took them wives of all which they chose . . . when the sons of God came in unto the daughters of men, and they bare children unto them, the same became mighty men which were of old, men of renown.[1]

Manifestly this is a mythological fragment of high antiquity. Avoiding the literal "sons of God" of the Hebrew, but quite possibly reflecting something like the original intent, the Septuagint Greek version used here the rendering *angeloi,* "angels." Moffatt's rendering follows this in the English, but the Chicago "American Translation" uses "sons of the gods." The new (1962) Jewish translation of *The Torah* has "divine beings."

The same phrasing appears in the simple folktale which provided the groundwork for the profoundly philosophical book of Job: "There was a day when the sons of God came to present themselves before the Lord." [2] Here again the Septuagint and the Moffatt versions have "angels," but this time the Chicago text shifts to "heavenly beings." In view of the fact that one of the characters included is the Satan, it is permissible to doubt that actual sonship to God

20

was meant to be attributed to any of them.

Wholly obscured in the "King James" English, but specifically "ye sons of God" in the Hebrew, is the address to "ye mighty" in Psalm 29:1. In this case the Septuagint stays with "sons of God," while Moffatt uses "angels," and Chicago and the Revised Standard "heavenly beings."

Though the "sons of God" phrasing is rare in the Old Testament, the identifying of these beings with the angels opens up wider areas of thought and expression. As we have seen in connection with the development of the doctrine of the Holy Spirit, we may regard the Biblical concept of the angels as a middle stage between the simple anthropomorphism of the earliest tales, when God used to run his own errands, and the spiritual realizations which were to come centuries later.

These heavenly "messengers" continue as more or less realistic figures into New Testament times, and even into New Testament thinking. There is no question, however, of their having been thought of as genetically related to the one God. The angels may be "divine beings" in the sense that they are other than human. They certainly are not at all on the same plane with, nor of the same nature as, the Creator whom they were created to serve.

Another kind of Old Testament reference to divine sonship is that which speaks of the nation of Israel in these terms. "When Israel was a child," Hosea recalls, "then I loved him, and called my son out of Egypt." (Needless to say, this is a historical reference to the Exodus from Egypt, not a predictive one to the flight from Bethlehem.) The Lord hath said unto me, "Thou art my son, this day have I begotten thee" may be thought of as addressed to the entire nation, or specially to the Davidic king as its representative.[3] In either case the relationship is treated as a moral rather than a biological one. Christian theologians may note also that in either case the sonship appears to be by adoption rather than by nature.

Thus the presence of beings called "sons of God" in the Hebrew Scriptures does no violence to the developing and at last fully developed Jewish monotheism. As angels the "sons of God" are but God's messengers, and thoroughly subordinate beings in the system of the universe. Humans accepted into a special relationship with the one God are his sons by way of a courtesy title, and not at all in essential character.

The genealogical mythology of Genesis 6, unique as it is in the Old Testament, does have recognizable and not uncommon parallels in the legends of ancient Greece. Here the "mighty men of old, men of renown," quite regularly were accounted for by the view that they were produced by the mating of divine males with human females. (On occasion it might be the other way, as in the carefully arranged marriage of the nymph Thetis to the human Peleus, resulting in the birth of Achilles; but this was a special and quite unusual case.)

Particularly the thunderer Zeus, "the father of gods and men," was credited with the paternity of those who were seen to be extraordinary persons. Heracles was the god's son by Alcmene, queen of Thebes. Dionysus, the god of wine, sprang from a union with Semele which destroyed the terrified young mother. Pollux of the "heavenly twins," and the matchlessly beautiful Helen of Sparta and later of Troy, were children of the swan-disguised Zeus and the bemused Leda. (The other twin, Castor, is said to have been the son of Leda's human husband Tyndareus, who also was the father of the queen Clytemnestra.) To the sequestered maid Danaë of Argos, Zeus appeared as a shower of gold, with the birth of Perseus as the consequence.

Alien and objectionable as were such Greek imaginings to the Jewish mind, they inevitably were familiar to that majority of the early Christian community which was Greek in its heritage. To say "Son of God" was for them not only to use a figure of speech for a celestial messenger, or for a person or a people peculiarly obedient to God, but also to explain, in a perfectly standard and accepted way, the character of a being recognized as very much out of the ordinary.

Finally in this connection we must notice again the idea of the *logos,* the divine Word as envisioned by the Greek philosophers and as adjusted to Jewish patterns by Philo. The concept originated, so far as we know, with the pioneering thinker Heraclitus (*ca.* 540-475 B.C.). Universally identified with his dictum that "all things change," [4] Heraclitus nevertheless regarded the ceaseless flux as operating within an inclusive and ordered unity. In what seems to have been the opening paragraph of his single book, quoted in its fullest known form by the third-century skeptic Sextus Empiricus and in part by Aristotle, Clement of Alexandria, and Hippolytus, Heraclitus asserts that

Although this Logos is eternally valid, yet men are unable

to understand it. . . . That is to say, although all things come to pass in accordance with this Logos, men seem to be quite without any experience of it—at least if they are judged in the light of such words and deeds as I am here setting forth.[5]

Similarly, in a related fragment, he declares that "although the Logos is common to all, most men live as if each of them had a private intelligence of his own." Almost identical with this, and quoted by the Stoic emperor Marcus Aurelius, is the line, "Although intimately connected with the Logos, men keep setting themselves against it." Yet again, in a sentence preserved by Hippolytus, we hear the warning, "Listening not to me but to the Logos, it is wise to acknowledge that all things are one." [6]

Epicharmus, a playwright of Syracuse who was born within a very few years of Heraclitus' death, almost certainly was borrowing from the Ephesian philosopher when he wrote,

> The Logos steers men and ever preserves them in the right way. Man has the power of calculation, but there is also the divine Logos. Human reasoning is sprung from the divine Logos, which furnishes to each man the passageway of both life and nourishment.[7]

Though he lived and ruled in the second century of the Christian era, the Roman Emperor Marcus Aurelius wrote in Greek and thought in terms of the Stoic philosophy. It is therefore fully legitimate to cite him as representing the thought world in which, and out of which, Christian thinking took its form. The Emperor pledged himself "to look to nothing else even momentarily except the Logos alone." He spoke of "the Logos held in common by gods and men," and of "the Logos ruling all things." The *logos spermatikos,* the generative Reason or life-giving Word, is that from which all things come and into which all shall return.[8]

Altogether in harmony with these expressions are the declarations about the Logos, made without specific reference either to Wisdom or to the Holy Spirit, which we find in the teaching of Philo. "The Logos of God," he says, "waters the virtues; for it is the source and spring of noble conduct." "The everlasting Logos of the eternal God," he believes, "is the very sure and staunch prop of the whole. . . . For the Father who begat Him constituted His word such a bond of the universe as nothing can break." [9]

Accepting their inevitably hybrid heritage from Athens and from Jerusalem, the early Christians seldom troubled consciously to ask themselves which of the constituent factors came from one source or from the other. We have seen that the background for Christian ideas of God is essentially Judaic. Perhaps surprisingly to some Christians of today, it is evident that the concept of the divine Spirit is principally Jewish too. It is no less clear that the identification of a Son of God, whether in the terms of mythology or in those of metaphysics, is much more largely Greek in its origins. The line from Philo just quoted above brings the whole pattern together, as does also the Fourth Gospel: "And the Word was made flesh, and dwelt among us, (and we beheld his glory, the glory as of the only begotten of the Father,) full of grace and truth." [10]

We turn now to observe how the Christian community made use of its varied inheritances of thought and faith, and what new structures of its own it built upon them. The enquiry begins with the New Testament, and continues through the developments of the first three Christian centuries. With their completion the groundwork at last was fully laid for the formulating of the doctrine of the Holy Trinity as we have known it.

The
Experience

LOGICAL and historical sequence have demanded that, in our study of the backgrounds of the doctrine of the Holy Trinity, the concept of the divine Spirit should be noted before that of the Son of God. As now we turn from the pre-Christian settings to the Christian experience itself, we find it advisable to make another and a different departure from the traditional order of discussion. The Son of God, whom we have noted third up to this point, now assumes the first position of all.

The specific and identifying Christian experience, that which made Christianity a vital entity and a viable force, was the encounter with Jesus of Nazareth. For many—if not for the majority of the early non-Jewish Christians— the actual object of their faith and worship, as the elder Arthur Cushman McGiffert pointed out more than a generation ago, was not the creating and ruling Lord of Israel, but the living and redeeming Christ.[1]

Early and next in the history of the Church, the sharp awareness of the divine presence was expressed in the doctrine of the Holy Spirit. "God the Father" was indeed central in Jesus' own thinking, and highly important in that of St. Paul. Jesus and Paul, however, had basic Jewish assumptions which were not shared by the Gentiles among the newly converted. In the course of time the systematizing theologians restored the "First Person" of the Trinity to formal primacy. For many believers, however, in all the centuries, the concept of Jesus as Lord has remained the real center of their faith.

We shall examine first, therefore, the Christians' efforts to account for the experienced phenomenon of Jesus; then their growing apprehension of the divine presence and power in the Holy Ghost; and the finally, in this connection, the role of the historic God of Israel in Christian thinking and teaching.

IV. THE LORD INCARNATE

"I'd rather take my Christology from the New Testament," said the orator at a long-ago summer conference, "than from the Laymen's Report on Rethinking Missions."[1] In the question period a young clergyman rose to his full height of six feet plus.

"I was interested, sir," he began, "in your reference to taking your Christology from the New Testament. May I enquire, sir, whether by that you mean the adoptionist Christology of the second chapter of the Acts? or the Messianic Christology of St. Matthew? or the kenotic Christology of St. Paul in Philippians? or the Logos Christology of the prologue to the Fourth Gospel? Or, sir, just what do you mean?"

No clarifying reply was offered, for apparently no clear

thinking had been done. Yet clarity and discrimination are essential if we are at all to understand the Church's course of trial and error and achievement as it sought to define in words the nature of its encounter with the Man of Galilee. The question of the young cleric will serve as a passably satisfactory outline for the enquiry now to be made.*

It was not with theory, but with experience, that the Christian faith began: not with impersonal dogma, but with personal impact. It was inevitable, nonetheless, that they who had known the experience should try to tell about it and to account for it. They wanted to identify its nature, to comprehend its meaning, to place it relevantly within their existing patterns of thought.

The essential dependability of St. Luke's report of St. Peter's preaching, in Acts 2, is argued by the fact that this is an obviously primitive and undeveloped interpretation which here is ascribed to the apostle. The start is by no means with a pre-existent being, nor even with a pre-designated one. It is simply with "Jesus of Nazareth, a man approved of God." There follows a brief recitation of the ministry, the death, and the resurrection. "Therefore," ends the argument, "let all the house of Israel know assuredly, that God hath made that same Jesus, whom ye crucified, both Lord and Christ." [2] "God hath made," one notes, not by advance decree, but "therefore": that is, after the event, and because of the quality of the life which has been lived.

---

* Let me make it clear that the questioner was not the present writer. He happened to be one of my former students, and I was proud of him. I have continued to be proud of him as I have seen him rise to leadership and distinction in his denomination.

This adoptionist approach is typically Jewish in its mood. It makes no attempt at metaphysical speculation. It but reacts to a practical situation. It is not surprising that the Ebionites, the Judaistic and Judaizing Christian sect of the years to follow, held to an adoptionist Christology throughout all their history.[3]

Adoptionism was too simple an answer, and one indeed too trivial, to satisfy most of those who realized the momentous nature of Jesus' presence among men. Surely it must have been not as an afterthought of God, but by his conscious forethought, that the Master was exalted above all his earthly fellows. Such an exaltation was provided for, still within the framework of historic Judaism, by the expectation of the coming Messiah.

The Messiah (*mashiach* = "anointed") was the divinely chosen king of Israel. When the actual kingdom of Judah ceased to be, with the destruction of Jerusalem in 586 B.C., the term was transferred from the phenomenal and historic Davidic monarchy to an ideal and future one. The anointed of the Lord would be the redeemer of the nation from its captivity, the restorer of its glories, the destroyer of its enemies.

Two major types of Messianic concept, and one minority one, are to be distinguished. At first the deliverer was thought of in purely human terms, as a warrior and governor such as all monarchs were expected to be. Even the Persian conqueror Cyrus is spoken of as the Lord's anointed, and so also are the "restoration" governor and high priest, Zerubbabel and Joshua. Four hundred years later, the brief triumph of the Maccabees suggested the union of kingship and supreme priesthood in a single personality.[4]

Military and political means, even though divinely sanctioned and assisted, proved to be ineffective. Not a human general, but a supernatural deliverer, seemed to many of those suffering under alien tyranny to be what they needed. Such a being makes his first notable appearance in the vision of Daniel:

> I saw in the night visions, and, behold, one like the Son of man came with the clouds of heaven, and came to the Ancient of days, and they brought him near before him.
> And there was given him dominion, and glory, and a kingdom, that all people, nations, and languages, should serve him: his dominion is an everlasting dominion, which shall not pass away, and his kingdom that which shall not be destroyed.[5]

The extra-canonical Jewish apocalypses further developed this concept, and made it normative for much of the Jewish community. In the Ethiopic Enoch the "Son of Man" is specifically identified as "the anointed," the Messiah.[6] The relationship between this type of Messianism and the early Christian expectation of the "second coming" of the Lord is evident. Manifestly Jesus had not been either a general or a governor. He had done nothing visible to "restore again the kingdom to Israel."[7] He certainly had done no appearing on the clouds of heaven.

How then, asked any reasonably informed Jew, could Jesus be thought by anyone to be the Messiah? The Christian, who on quite other and much more significant grounds had accepted and declared the Messianic identity, had only one quick and simple way out. "Not yet," he replied to his challenger; "not yet, but inevitably very soon."

What were the other and prior grounds for the Messianic identification? In general they were simply those of Jewish thought and hope. The Messiah was to be the supreme man, the king of men. No higher category, other than that of God himself, existed for the Jewish mind. When therefore a supreme man presented himself in a Jewish community, those who recognized his supremacy almost inescapably saw it as his Messiahship.

There was also available to the early Christians, as still there is to us, a non-military, non-magical, and non-majority view of the Messiah which made the equation of Jesus with him more simple and much more lasting. This had been explicitly set forth in a late addition to the book of Zechariah. It conveyed perhaps the only Old Testament prediction which Jesus chose deliberately and literally to fulfill:

> Rejoice greatly, O daughter of Zion; shout, O daughter of Jerusalem: behold, thy King cometh unto thee: he is just, and having salvation; lowly, and riding upon an ass, and upon a colt the foal of an ass.
> And I will cut off the chariot from Ephraim, and the horse from Jerusalem, and the battle bow shall be cut off: and he shall speak peace unto the heathen: and his dominion shall be from sea even to sea, and from the river even to the ends of the earth.[8]

This lowly king, riding on the peasant's workaday donkey rather than on the warrior's snorting charger, was specifically a Messiah of humility and of peace. This sort of

Messiah, and this sort only, Jesus seems to have been willing to be. Many of his followers, however, were content neither with this simplicity in fact nor with this normality in fulfillment.

In standard rabbinic fashion the Gospel of St. Matthew tries to establish the Messianic identity by proof-texting from the Scriptures. Several of the choices are unfortunate: a birth which had occurred more than seven centuries earlier, a flight from Egypt which actually belongs to the Exodus of the Israelites under Moses, and a "slaughter of the innocents" which relates to the later Exile in Babylon.[9] The evangelist's arguments do not establish his point. His using them yet makes clear his conviction: the conviction of a believing Jew that the Lord's anointed verily had come in the person of Jesus.

That conviction, as we have noted, carried over also into the apocalyptic aspects of the Messianic hope. At least in the earlier years of his mission St. Paul accepted these concomitants of the Jewish Christology,[10] though he said little about them in his later writings. The same expectant mood permeates the Revelation of St. John, though the particular word "Christ," the Greek equivalent for "Messiah," appears in this book with surprising infrequency (four times in the twenty-two chapters).[11]

It is just this matter of Greek equivalence which we must consider next. "Thou art the Christ," the Messiah, cries the Jewish disciple Peter shortly before the Transfiguration. It is not Judaism, but Hellenism, which adds "the son of the living God" in St. Matthew's transcription, and which gives us "the Christ of God" in St. Luke's.[12]

The Messiah had high relevance for one brought up in Judaism. He had none at all for those whose heritage was Gentile. They knew little of Jewish history, and they cared nothing about Jewish national hopes and dreams.

It befell, therefore, that *Christos,* "anointed," the literal Greek translation of the Jewish *Mashiach,* "Messiah," lost rapidly any denotative significance. It became for even the earliest of Greek Christians what it has remained for most of their successors (including Britons and Americans), an added name for Jesus with almost no meaning attached. For a Greek to find a real equivalent, a glorifying of the observed and experienced Jesus comparable to what the Jew had found in calling him Messiah, it was necessary to turn to categories in which the Greek mind could operate comfortably.

The chief one of these, as already has been suggested, was that of "son of God." That this was not necessarily thought of in biological terms is evident from the fact that the expression is quite as common in the New Testament books which make no reference to the Virgin Birth, as it is in the Gospels of St. Matthew and St. Luke. Whether the sections of those two works which speak of the birth from the Blessed Virgin are authentic parts of the original texts is a matter of dispute. Since they do stand early in the existing documents, however, and since unquestionably they reflect the idea of a special divine sonship, they should be examined now.

Neither the representation in St. Matthew nor that in St. Luke actually alleges parthenogenesis. "That which is conceived in her," St. Matthew's angel tells Joseph, "is of the Holy Ghost." Thus also, according to our present text of St. Luke, the angel Gabriel promises Mary herself that

> The Holy Ghost shall come upon thee, and the power of the Highest shall overshadow thee: therefore also that holy thing which shall be born of thee shall be called the Son of God.[13]

Manifestly this is, in both cases, an assertion not of virginity but specifically of divine paternity.

That this view was not upsetting to the mind of a second-century Gentile Christian is shown by St. Justin Martyr, writing about A.D. 155:

> In saying that the Logos, who is the first offspring of God, was born for us without sexual union, as Jesus Christ our Teacher, and that he was crucified and died and after rising again ascended into heaven we introduce nothing new beyond [what you say of] those whom you call sons of Zeus. You know how many sons of Zeus the writers whom you honor speak of . . .

Here follows a list including Hermes, Asclepius, Dionysus, Heracles, the Dioscuri, Perseus, and Bellerophon. Then, after some strictures on the personal morals of Zeus, the apologist continues:

> Now if God's Son, who is called Jesus, were only an ordinary man, he would be worthy because of his wisdom to be called Son of God, for all authors call God father of men and gods. When we say, as before, that he was begotten by God as the Word of God in a unique manner beyond ordinary birth, this should be no strange thing for you who speak of Hermes as the announcing word from God. If somebody objects that he was crucified, this is in common with the sons of Zeus, as you call them, who suffered, as previously listed. . . . If we declare

that he was born of a virgin, you should consider this something in common with Perseus.[14]

Only a little further on in the same work, Justin seems to repent him of having accepted so much of the pagan mythologies. He tries now to distinguish between the cases of the Greek heroes and that of Jesus. "If (Mary) had had intercourse with anyone," he says, "she would not have been a virgin; but God's power, coming upon the Virgin, overshadowed her, and caused her to conceive while still remaining a virgin."[15] This certainly is introducing something "new beyond what you say of those whom you call sons of Zeus." Whether it is any more comprehensible, or whether in any way it can be made to seem consistent with Justin's previous arguing, each reader of the apologist will have to determine for himself.

The phrasings of the early adumbrations of the Apostles' Creed likewise leave room for acceptance of the Greek mythological interpretation. The "Old Roman Symbol," as set forth by Marcellus of Ancyra in A.D. 337, reads, "his only Son our Lord, born of the Holy Ghost and Mary the Virgin."[16] About A.D. 400 Rufinus of Aquilea used the form "born of the Holy Ghost from Mary the Virgin."[17] Nor is there any categorical declaration of parthenogenesis in the received form of the Creed as regularly we say it today: "Conceived by the Holy Ghost, born of the Virgin Mary."

Much more important than any biological representation of Jesus' sonship to God are the moral and spiritual judgments which the early Christian thinkers based upon their observation of Jesus' character and life. Not surprisingly, one of the critical examples is to be found in the Hellenistic Jewish, and clearly Philonic, "epistle to the Hebrews." The Son is infinitely higher than the angels, and he is "crowned with glory and honour" because he has been made "perfect through sufferings." The lawgiver Moses was a servant, but the Christ was "a son over his own house." And "though he were a Son, yet learned he obedience by the things which he suffered." This Son of God is assumed to be eternal in his own person, and he is declared to have been God's agent in the making of the worlds.[18]

Here already we catch echoes of the creative Logos of the Stoics, and something like a preview of the prologue to the Fourth Gospel. Before we turn to the Johannine treatment, however, we must notice St. Paul's classic assertion of our Lord's preexistence in the idea of the *kenosis*, the self-emptying. Here the King James rendering is inaccurate, in its reading "thought it not robbery to be equal with God." Better translated in the Revised Standard Version, the passage runs:

> Have this mind among yourselves, which you have in Christ Jesus, who, though he was in the form of God, did not count equality with God a thing to be grasped, but emptied himself, taking the form of a servant, being born in the likeness of men. And being found in human form he humbled himself and became obedient unto death, even death on a cross. Therefore God hath highly exalted him and bestowed on him the name which is above every name, that at the name of Jesus every knee should bow, in heaven and on earth and under the earth, and every tongue confess that Jesus Christ is Lord, to the glory of God the Father.[19]

St. Paul did not write the letter to the Hebrews, and there are obvious differences between the two Christian authors not only in literary style but also in theological emphases. Nevertheless they are altogether at one as to both the metaphysical and the moral character of the Son's relation to the Father. He existed before all the worlds, he shared in the divine glory throughout eternity, but he authenticated his mission and his person ultimately and in the time dimension ("in these last days") by his humiliation as a servant, learning obedience by the things which he suffered.

There is less of emphasis on the humiliation, though no less on the earthly incarnation, in the opening section of the Fourth Gospel. As has long been recognized and often said, no Stoic would have had any difficulty at all with the first five verses of St. John:

> In the beginning was the Logos, and the Logos was with God, and the Logos was God. The same was in the beginning with God. All things were made by him: and without him was not any thing made that was made. In him was life; and the life was the light of men. And the light shineth in darkness; and the darkness comprehended it not.

This could have been written by the pioneering Heraclitus, by any Stoic, or by the Hellenizing Philo.[20]

But suddenly Christian uniqueness breaks through. It is hinted in the reference to the historic St. John the Baptist. It voices itself clearly in the assurance that those who received the Word were qualified to "become the sons of God." It rings out climactically and gloriously in the triumphant "the Logos was made flesh, and dwelt among us."

A Stoic could not have said this. A Greek-oriented Christian, reflecting on what he had heard and seen and "handled" of the Word of life, simply had to say it.[21]

This Ephesian author's successors, the apologists in the second century and the Alexandrian teachers in the third, unanimously identified the concept of the Logos with that of the Son. "The Father sent the Logos to appear to the world," says the anonymous Letter to Diognetus, whose addressee may have been the tutor of Marcus Aurelius. "This is the eternal one, who today is accounted a Son." [22] Here we find ourselves remembering Hebrews and Philippians also, for the "today" is after the historic *kenosis* and the incarnation, and the accounting because of them.

Already we have noted Justin's phrasing, "the Logos, who is the first offspring of God." Elsewhere he says, "Jesus Christ alone really was begotten as Son of God, being his Logos and First begotten and Power." And again, "The first Power after God the Father and Master of all, even [his] Son, is the Logos." [23]

Some twenty years later the Athenian Christian Athenagoras teaches that "the Son of God is his Logos in idea and in actuality . . . the Son of God is the mind and Logos of the Father." (Between those two clauses there stands an unmistakable statement of Trinitarian faith, which I defer for later quotation and discussion.) In the next generation Clement of Alexandria says, "The Son is the power of God, as being the original Logos of the Father, prior to all created things." One generation more, and Clement's catechetical successor Origen appears, in the recently discovered "Dialogue with Heraclides," as asking for further defining of the affirmation that "his [God's] Logos is the Son of the living God." [24]

Total definition eluded both Heraclides and his interlocutor Origen, and it still eludes us. What is clear, and ever has been clear to those with readiness to see, is that each man and each group within the Christian community depended upon one or another particular cultural heritage in the effort to account for the human experience with the Christ. Adoption, Messiahship, sonship, *kenosis,* Logos: none of these is final, but each of them is meaningful in its own right. Ultimately all of them are true, if by truth we understand accordance with reality.

The single fact of Jesus gave rise to the miscellany of Christian doctrine. We shall not regret the miscellany, for it demonstrates that the single fact was by no means a simple one. Through all of the miscellany we may come the better to envisage for ourselves the suffering and redeeming servant, the Son of God, the Logos made flesh and dwelling among us. In all of it the Christian view of God includes, in its very essence, the conviction that God for men's sake became man.

V. THE LORD IN RESIDENCE

The "transmuted eschatology" of the Fourth Gospel points to an identity even while it asserts a distinction. "I will pray the Father," says Jesus in his last conversation with the disciples before the arrest and trial, "and he shall give you another Comforter, that he may abide with you for ever; even the Spirit of truth." Then, almost in the next breath, he assures them, "I will not leave you comfortless: I will come to you." [1]

His apparent equation of the Spirit with the Son stands late, however, in the story of New Testament doctrine. Prior to it is the narrative of the visible and audible descent of the Holy Ghost, in Acts 2. Prior to that, in turn, are most of the Gospel references. Earlier than any of these are the authentic letters of the apostle Paul.[2]

In the beginning of what is probably the earliest extant specimen of his correspondence, Paul declares that "our gospel came not unto you in word only, but in power, and in the Holy Ghost." The Spirit controls the apostle's message, "not in the words which man's wisdom teacheth, but which the Holy Ghost teacheth." Thus also "no man can say that Jesus is the Lord, but by the Holy Ghost." [3]

The gifts of the Spirit are not only intellectual, however,
> For to one is given the Spirit of wisdom; to another the word of knowledge by the same Spirit; to another faith by the same Spirit; to another the gifts of healing by the same Spirit; to another the working of miracles; to another prophecy; to another discerning of spirits; to another divers kinds of tongues; to another the interpretation of tongues: but all these worketh that one and the selfsame Spirit, dividing to every man severally as he will.

Climactically in this passage, the Spirit, besides being the distributor of individual gifts, is also the unifying force of the whole Christian community: "For by one Spirit are we all baptized into one body, whether we be Jews or Gentiles, whether we be bond or free; and have been all made to drink into one Spirit." This last surely supplies the essential interpreting of "the communion of the Holy Ghost" in a later farewell to the same Corinthian friends.[4]

In two of his most notable flights of eloquence the apostle contrasts the Spirit with the now superseded Law. "If ye be led of the Spirit," he tells the Galatians,

> ye are not under the law. Now the works of the flesh are manifest, which are these: Adultery, fornication, uncleanness, lasciviousness, idolatry, witchcraft, hatred, variance, emulations, wrath, strife, seditions, heresies, envyings, murders, drunkenness, revellings, and such like.

Not "works" now, but "the fruit of the Spirit," are "love, joy, peace, longsuffering, gentleness, goodness, faith, meekness, temperance: against such there is no law."[5]

It follows that the Spirit is the giver of the Christian's freedom. The human "epistle of Christ" is "written not with ink, but with the Spirit of the living God." The true "new testament," the new covenant of God with man, is "not of the letter, but of the spirit": not a collection of documents, but a vital personal experience. "The spirit giveth life" is less than an adequate rendering of the next line. What the Greek actually says is, "The Spirit makes alive" (*to de pneuma zōopoiei*); and there is no reason here for the King James' lower-case spelling.

The conclusion of this matter is that "The Lord is the Spirit," which sounds almost like the identification which we have noted in the Fourth Gospel. Immediately following, however, are two occurrences of "the Spirit of the Lord," suggesting rather a clear distinction between the two. The passage ends, "Where the Spirit of the Lord is, there is liberty." A long-ago conjecture of the textual editors Westcott and Hort would read this rather, and by the changing only of a single letter, "Where the Spirit is Lord, there is liberty." [6]

Not all the gifts of the Spirit are easy to deal with, however. In particular the "divers kinds of tongues" had created difficulties in the Corinthian church. It is patent that St. Paul knew nothing of the gift of tongues as a gift of languages, such as is represented in Acts 2. The King James translators inserted "unknown" before "tongue" in an effort to harmonize the two concepts, but without authority in the original. What the apostle said was simply, "He who speaks in a tongue speaks not to men, but to God. No one understands him." It is of course for this reason that he concludes, "Yet in the church I had rather speak five words with my understanding that by my voice I might teach others also, than ten thousand words in a tongue." [7]

The ecstatic but incomprehensible utterances called "glossolalia" were not unknown in the Hellenistic cults of the time. Whether the phenomenon was one widely spread among the earliest Christian groups, or whether it was concentrated in Corinth, is not certainly to be known. The latter seems on the whole the more probable, as St. Paul nowhere discusses the issue in any of his other letters. Nor does any other New Testament writer allude to it, except the author of Acts in his account of the day of Pentecost and in one passing later reference.[8]

The Pentecostal episode is a special case, and in some of its details not a very helpful one. The conviction that the very Spirit of God had entered into the primitive Christian community is evident. The particular manifestation of a miraculous or even magical linguistic fluency is less convincing and much less edifying.

The attempt to rationalize by saying that anyway it took only Greek and Aramaic to cover the situation for a crowd of travelers in the first-century Middle East robs the narrative of its obvious intent to record a most extraordinary episode. That intent, however, flies in the face of everything we know about the "gift of tongues" in New Testament times and ever since. At the best we may regard this story as a symbolic reference to the universal spreading of the Gospel through the Spirit's agency.

The living presence of the Holy Spirit needed no external wonder for its authentication. Throughout the book of Acts we find the Church persuaded of that divine presence, and living in and by it both individually and collectively. Jesus, on the mount of the ascension, promises the baptism with the Holy Ghost. It is the Holy Ghost who qualifies St. Peter to speak boldly to the chief priests, and who gives like courage to all the assembled company of believers. The Holy Ghost is the strengthener also of St. Stephen at the moment of his martyrdom.[9]

In the case of Simon, the sorcerer of Samaria, the gift of the Holy Ghost is denied because of his total lack of moral discernment. A reminiscence of the Old Testament duality of angels and the Spirit appears in the story of Philip "the Evangelist" and the Ethiopian eunuch: "the angel of the Lord spake unto Philip," but immediately afterward, "then the Spirit said unto Philip . . ."[10]

The Holy Ghost authenticates the conversion of the

Gentiles at Caesarea, even before their baptism. He assigns Barnabas and Saul to their pioneering mission overseas. He is introduced to the followers of St. John the Baptist at Ephesus. He has appointed the "overseers" (*episkopous*, "bishops") there. Once more at Caesarea, he inspires the prophet Agabus with foreknowledge of Paul's fate.[11]

No doubt because Jesus himself is the central personage of the narratives in the first three Gospels (called "Synoptic") the Spirit as such receives relatively little mention in them. John the Baptist does promise that the coming one will "baptize with the Holy Ghost." The Spirit then descends on Jesus (visibly or invisibly, depending on which Gospel one is reading), and soon drives (or leads) him into the wilderness.[12]

The most notable reference to the Spirit in the Synoptics is also the most puzzling: "He that shall blaspheme against the Holy Ghost hath never forgiveness, but is in danger of eternal damnation." [13] Just what is meant by this "sin against the Holy Ghost"? The difficulty of answering with certainty is intensified by the accounts of St. Matthew and St. Luke, for here that sin is categorically said to be much more grave than is rejection of "the Son of man." It is possible, but not very likely, that here "Son of man" was intended to mean no more than "man" or "human being." If, as is more probable, the reference indeed is to Jesus himself, the distinction must be made on the difference between recognition and non-recognition of the divine in him. In these terms, what is unforgivable is to repudiate God's Spirit when he has been identified and recognized as such.

"He that hath an ear, let him hear what the Spirit saith unto the churches." What the Spirit says to the seven churches, in the second and third chapters of the Revelation of St. John, is not altogether complimentary. He is less a Comforter than a Discomforter in his challenges to Ephesus and Pergamos, Thyatira and Sardis, Philadelphia and especially the lukewarm Laodicea. Only Smyrna escapes without something of a scolding.

The exile of Patmos is qualified to transmit these messages because he himself "was in the Spirit on the Lord's day." Near the close of the book again he is "carried . . . away in the spirit to a great and high mountain," that he may see the "holy Jerusalem, descending out of heaven from God." And so at the last "the Spirit and the bride say, Come," the indwelling Lord and his Church uniting in the invitation to everyone who hears.[14]

The Spirit is scarcely more prominent in the early chapters of the Fourth Gospel than he is in the Synoptics. The author is clear that "the Holy Ghost was not yet given; because that Jesus was not yet glorified." Man nevertheless must be "born of water and of the Spirit" if he is to enter the kingdom of God. God himself is spirit, and possibly "a Spirit" withal, in the conversation with the woman of Samaria. "The Spirit is the life-maker," even as St. Paul has told the Corinthians.[15] This is all, until we come to the fourteenth chapter.

The only really intensive discussion of the nature and mission of the Spirit in all the Gospel literature is in this Johannine account of the conversation after the Last Supper. As we saw at the beginning of this enquiry into the doctrine, there is a hint here that the Spirit's promised coming is to be identified with the Lord's own return. Still clearer, however, and by no necessity contradicting this, is the representation of the Spirit as taking Jesus' place functionally in the life of the disciples.

The "Comforter" of course is not a tranquilizer, but the strengthener, the invigorator. "Com-fort" is "strength with," even though the Unabridged Dictionary now marks that meaning as obsolete. In the Greek the Comforter is the *parakletos,* an advocate, an intercessor, a defender. The New English Bible uses "Advocate," and the Revised Standard "Counselor." What the Comforter does, and will do, is set forth throughout the discourse.

The Paraclete will "teach you all things, and bring all things to your remembrance, whatsoever I have said unto you." "He will reprove the world of sin" (the Discomforter again), and "he will guide you into all truth." "He shall glorify me," says Jesus, "for he shall receive of mine, and shall shew it unto you." Here again is the suggestion of identity in function, if not necessarily in person. And the theme of identity recurs with "A little while, and ye shall not see me; and again, a little while, and ye shall see me." [16]

All of this is summed up, and the character and mission of the Holy Spirit specified, in "ye know him; for he dwelleth with you, and shall be in you." [17] The Holy Ghost was recognized as the Lord in residence among his people, and in the mind and heart of each individual in their number. This, according to St. John, Jesus had promised. This—the primitive Church believed and was convinced it knew—

assuredly had come to pass.

The early Fathers contribute little that is new in their references to the Spirit. They acknowledge his activity in the life of the Christian community. They accept and emphasize the Old Testament view that the Spirit inspired both Moses and the prophets. What is something of an innovation here is a stress on Biblical infallibility which is quite at odds with the free treatment of the Scriptures in the teaching of Jesus and in the letters of Paul. "The Spirit used (the prophets) just as a flute player blows on a flute," says Athenagoras to his pagan readers.[18]

An extreme development from the Corinthian excitements of Paul's time was the movement known as Montanism. Montanus was a Phrygian of the middle of the second century. According to the fourth-century historian Eusebius, Montanus

> was one of the recent converts, and he became possessed of a spirit, and suddenly began to rave in a kind of ecstatic trance, and to babble in a jargon, prophesying in a manner contrary to the custom of the Church which had been handed down by tradition from the earliest times. . . .
>
> And he also stirred up two women and filled them with the bastard spirit so that they uttered demented, absurd, and irresponsible sayings.

These two women are named by Hippolytus as "Priscilla and Maximilla . . . whom they hold to be prophetesses, asserting that into them the Paraclete spirit entered." [19]

The pioneer Latin Christian writer, Tertullian of Carthage, moved gradually into the Montanist camp. His writings from about A.D. 210, beginning with his *De*

Anima, "Of the Soul," are products of his Montanist conclusions. "We have among us now a sister," he testifies, "who has been granted gifts of revelations, which she experiences during the Sunday services through ecstatic vision in the Spirit." Tertullian unhesitatingly accepts the "new prophets" as assured authority, even against the dicta of the official Church. "As a minister," he asks,

> who are you to grant forgiveness, and by what right? . . . In the new prophets I have the Paraclete himself saying, "The Church can pardon sins, but I will not do it, lest they commit other sins." [20]

Farther eastward along the North African coast, a quieter voice is that of Origen of Alexandria. "I pray as a man," he says,

> (for I do not hold that I am able of my own self to treat of prayer) before I begin to speak on the subject of prayer, that the Holy Spirit may be vouchsafed to me, so that a very full and spiritual word may be bestowed upon me.

The treatise ends, and surely in a presaging of Trinitarianism,

> And having begun by glorifying God it is fitting to conclude and bring the prayer to an end by glorifying him, hymning and glorifying the Father of the universe through Jesus Christ in the Holy Spirit, "to whom be the glory for ever." [21]

Origen was writing some ninety years before the Council of Nicea. Just where he stood in his thinking about the inner relationships of the Godhead is debatable. What is undeniable is that for him the Holy Spirit was real and vital and present, among men and in his own life. That had been the continuing faith and experience of the Church from the earliest days, and even before that in the life of Judaism. There is no reason to discard that faith in these latter days of Christianity, for we have no reason ourselves to deny or to doubt the experience.

VI. THE LORD ETERNAL

Jesus was a Jew. This was enough to guarantee that the focal point both of his theological thinking and of his religious allegiance should be the Lord God of Israel. That he himself was the incarnate revelation of God was a conclusion of the Church, a conclusion which we as Christians share. That the revealer should turn attention away from the one he was revealing could not have entered Jesus' mind.

Nor are we justified in holding, as have some, that the God in whom Jesus believed, and whom he revealed, was in any essential quality different from the God in which the Jews had believed and whom they sought to serve. Jesus came not to destroy the Law, or the Prophets, but to fulfil them.[1] In particular, he reflected and asserted those estimates of God's moral character and those ethical demands which had been set forth by the prophets of Israel and Judah.

As we have noted already, Jesus regarded "the Spirit of the Lord" as having assigned him, in fulfilment of a late exilic promise,

> to preach the gospel to the poor . . . to heal the broken-hearted, to preach deliverance to the captives, and recov-

ering of sight to the blind, to set at liberty them that are
bruised, to preach the acceptable year of the Lord.[2]
St. Matthew quotes him twice, in rapid succession, as citing
Hosea's "I desired mercy, and not sacrifice." [3] With the
first Isaiah he recognizes that "this people honoureth
(God) with their lips, but their heart is far from (him)."
And he follows this with a characteristically prophetic
insistence on moral over ceremonial righteousness.[4]

It is this same view of God which leads to the joining
together of the two commandments in the "Summary of
the Law": "Thou shalt love the Lord thy God. . . . Thou
shalt love thy neighbour as thyself." Once more it is a
wholly prophetic judgment which is pronounced by the
enquiring scribe, and approved by Jesus, in the response,

> . . . there is one God; and there is none other but he: and
> to love him with all the heart, and with all the under-
> standing, and with all the soul, and with all the strength,
> and to love his neighbour as himself, is more than all
> whole burnt offerings and sacrifices.[5]

A God whom one can love is of necessity one who
himself loves his people. This however is implied, more
than it is asserted, in the Synoptic materials. God's love is
shown in his willingness to forgive men their trespasses.
Coupled with this, however, is yet another demand of the
prophetic cast, that they who would be forgiven shall
themselves be ready to forgive.[6]

If they do not forgive, they need not expect anything
of divine favor. It is undeniable that the first three Gospels present Jesus as recognizing a God of anger and
punishment in the same person as his God of love and
forgiveness. Gehenna was the Jerusalem city dump, and

in contemporary apocalyptic writings it had been identified as a most unhappy Sheol, the abiding place of the unrighteous dead. Effectively in the terminology of the time, Gehenna was what we would call "hell."

According to Jesus in the Synoptics, Gehenna is the destination of those who hold their fellows in contempt. It awaits those who surrender themselves to impure desire. It is not to be escaped by those who prove themselves to be "the children of them which killed the prophets." Not Gehenna specifically, but a fully equivalent "everlasting fire," is the fate of those who have failed to minister to the hungry, the thirsty, the strangers, the naked, the sick, and the imprisoned.[7] Thus Jesus is seen to align himself with the prophets not only in their ethical estimates but also in their moral indignation; and to assume with them that God himself shares and enforces these same value judgments.

As to any special personal relationship of Jesus to God, the Synoptic testimony is ambivalent. "If thou be the Son of God," says the tempter, "command that these stones be made bread." Jesus responds to this temptation, and to those which follow, with Old Testament injunctions that would apply to any faithful servant of God: "Man shall not live by bread alone, but by every word that proceedeth out of the mouth of God . . . Thou shalt not tempt the Lord thy God . . . Thou shalt worship the Lord thy God, and him only shalt thou serve." [8]

"Why do you call me good? [Jesus asks the 'rich young ruler'] There is none good but one, that is, God." The editor of St. Matthew, obviously unwilling to record this

self-derogation on Jesus' part, changed the question to,
"Why do you ask me about the good?" Oddly enough, this
softening was lost in later manuscripts, which assimilated
the text of St. Matthew again to the original Marcan form;
and so the King James version presents St. Matthew, inac-
curately, as being in accordance here with the other two
Synoptics.[9]

The story of the paralytic let down through the roof
seems categorically to assign to Jesus the divine authority
to forgive. The same authority is asserted, as it is challenged by the onlookers, in St. Luke's account of the
penitent woman in the house of Simon the Pharisee. On
the other hand, Jesus on the cross addresses to God a plea
for the forgiving of his persecutors. And on the cross, too,
according to St. Matthew, he utters the despairing cry,
"My God, my God, why hast thou forsaken me?" [10]

What may be regarded as the single "Johannine" passage in all the Synoptics appears in St. Matthew, without
any parallel in St. Mark or St. Luke:

> All things are delivered unto me of my Father: and no
> man knoweth the Son, but the Father; neither knoweth
> any man the Father, save the Son, and he to whomsoever
> the Son will reveal him.

Quite clearly the author of St. Mark does not share the
view that "all things" have been thus revealed. He quotes
Jesus as saying, "Of that day and that hour knoweth no
man, no, not the angels which are in heaven, neither the
Son, but the Father." [11]

"The Son" may be an exclusive identification, but "the
Father" is not a Father to this Son only. One of the numer-

ous Christian misapprehensions is the notion that the fatherhood of God was unknown in the Jewish tradition, and was announced to mankind only with the coming of Christianity. The Hebrew names Joab and Abijah, Eliab and Abiel, "Jahveh-Father" and "God-Father," all attest the very early date of the concept. "A father of the fatherless," says one Psalmist, "is God in his holy habitation." "Like as a father pitieth his children," another Hebrew poet assures us, "so the Lord pitieth them that fear him." [12]

"I am a father to Israel," says the Lord through Jeremiah. "Thou, O Lord, art our father, our redeemer," declares a post-exilic seer. This God, according to the last of the Old Testament books, is at least the father of all Israel if not of all mankind: "Have we not all one father? hath not one God created us?" [13]

"Father" nevertheless is a much more usual designation for God in the New Testament than it is in the Old. Among the Synoptics it occurs the most frequently in St. Matthew. It is in the Fourth Gospel, however, that the divine fatherhood is the most regularly mentioned and the most thoroughly defined.

God here is the Father of all. At the same time, there can be no doubt that this Gospel thinks also of a very special relationship between the Father and the unique Son who is Jesus. When the Jews challenge him, because he "said also that God was his Father, making himself equal with God," he accepts the charge unhesitatingly. "The Father loveth the Son," he replies. "He that honoureth not the Son honoureth not the Father which hath sent him." [14]

In the final Johannine discourse this Sonship passes almost into complete identification. "If ye had known me, ye should have known my Father also: and from henceforth ye know him, and have seen him." Philip's puzzled protest brings but a repetition and an intensification: "Have I been so long time with you, and yet hast thou not known me, Philip? he that hath seen me hath seen the Father; and how sayest thou then, Shew us the Father?" [15]

This, however, must be recognized as a comparatively late development in the Christian reaction to the person of Jesus. For St. Paul "the light of the knowledge of the glory of God" indeed is given "in the face of Jesus Christ." The Son is "the image of the invisible God, the firstborn of every creature." [16] Nevertheless the apostle is much too thoroughly a Jew to allow his faith in the Christ to make him forget the eternal Lord of Israel.

"The true and living God" is clearly distinguished from "his Son from heaven." It is "God, even our Father, which hath loved us, and hath given us everlasting consolation and good hope through grace." "Because ye are sons," St. Paul tells the Galatians, "God hath sent forth the Spirit of his Son into your hearts, crying, Abba, Father." "God is faithful," he assures the Christians of Corinth, "by whom ye were called unto the fellowship of his Son Jesus Christ our Lord." "Blessed be God," he begins another letter to them, "even the Father of our Lord Jesus Christ, the Father of mercies, and the God of all comfort." [17]

Paul's later epistles are no less categorical about the primacy of the Father. "The gospel of God" is that

> concerning his Son Jesus Christ our Lord, which was
> made of the seed of David according to the flesh; and
> declared to be the Son of God with power, according to
> the Spirit of holiness, by the resurrection from the dead.

Standing alone, those verses in Romans might even be interpreted as consonant with an adoptionist Christology. The Colossians are called on to give

> thanks unto the Father, which hath made us meet to be
> partakers of the inheritance of the saints in light: who
> hath delivered us from the power of darkness, and hath
> translated us into the kingdom of his dear Son . . . who
> is the image of the invisible God.

The salutation to Philemon is "Grace to you, and peace, from God our Father and the Lord Jesus Christ," and the apostle thanks his God, "making mention of thee always in my prayers, hearing of thy love and faith, which thou hast toward the Lord Jesus, and toward all saints." [18]

Most strikingly of all, the famous section on the *kenosis* concludes:

> Wherefore God also hath highly exalted him, and given
> him a name which is above every name: that at the
> name of Jesus every knee should bow, of things in
> heaven, and things in earth, and things under the earth;
> and that every tongue should confess that Jesus Christ is
> Lord, to the glory of God the Father.[19]

That is to say, both the self-humbling and the exaltation of Christ Jesus are directed to exhibit and to assure "the glory of God the Father." This surely is very different from the interpretation provided by Dr. Thomas Altizer, in which the *kenosis* issues not at all in God's glorification, but precisely in his death.[20]

Though the whole drive of the epistle to the Hebrews

is to demonstrate the superiority of the new covenant to the former one, there can be no question but that for this author, too, the God of both the covenants is the same. The opening paragraph speaks of the God who has revealed himself both in the past and in the present, and the final benediction runs, "The God of peace, that brought again from the dead our Lord Jesus . . . make you perfect in every good work to do his will . . . through Jesus Christ." The great anthem of faith, which of course owes much to the praise of "famous men" in the apocryphal book of Ecclesiasticus, refers as clearly as does its model to faith in the God of Israel. It is only after the "wherefore" at the conclusion, which Robert Stephens in 1551 quite properly set off as the beginning of a new chapter, that Jesus is mentioned at all.[21]

All this, however, reflects the Jewish orientation shared by Jesus, Paul, and the somewhat Hellenized but still Jewish writer of Hebrews. It does not represent the approach of the Gentile Christian who had no personal background in Judaism. The primordial God of Israel was not immediately condemned to death, as he has been by a few of our contemporary theologians, but he was effectively ignored.

In the formal triad of philosophical Hinduism, Brahma is the Creator, Vishnu the Preserver, and Shiva the Destroyer. No doubt because the work of creation is considered to be a *fait accompli,* whereas preservation is seen to continue and destruction regularly to occur, popular Hindu piety has concentrated heavily on the second and third figures at the expense of the first. It is said that in all India there is only one shrine dedicated to Brahma in his own person. Vaishnavite worship, in contrast, is the dominant religious expression in the Indian North, and Shivaite devotion in the southerly regions.

In much the same way, the experience of the early non-Jewish Christians had been centered on the historic person of Jesus, and in the immediate presence of the Holy Spirit, to the substantial ignoring of the timeless Creator God of Israel. Just as Jewish Messianism had no meaning for a Roman or a Greek, and so in Hellenistic Christianity had to yield to the concept of the Son of God or of the Logos; thus also traditional Jewish theology seemed to have no necessary relevance to Gentile Christian devotion. At first this appears to have been nothing more than a fairly natural neglect. Ere long, however, it became in some circles an active opposition issuing in an explicit rejection.

These circles were those called "Gnostic." Gnosticism was identified long ago, by Adolf Harnack, as "an acute Hellenizing of Christianity." [22] The most vigorous and most insistent of these deniers of the Jewish God was the sea captain Marcion from Pontus. Because this geographical and ideological voyager quickly was repudiated as a heretic, we know him only through the charges hurled by his Christian opponents and condemners. Irenaeus of Lyons is authority for one famous anecdote. "Do you know us?" Marcion asked Polycarp, the aged Bishop of Smyrna and sometime pupil of the Fourth Evangelist. "I know you," the old man replied, "the first-born of Satan." [23] Despite the obvious prejudices, however, there seems to be no reason to doubt the substantial accuracy of the orthodox reporting of Marcion's views.

"By the help of the demons," says Justin,

> he has made many in every race of men to blaspheme and to deny God the Maker of the universe, professing that there is another who is greater and has done greater things than he.[24]

Irenaeus speaks of one Cerdon, who "taught that the God preached by the Law and the Prophets was not the Father of our Lord Jesus Christ." "After him," Irenaeus continues,

> came Marcion of Pontus, who developed his teaching, shamelessly blaspheming the God whom the Law and the Prophets proclaimed, describing him as the author of evils, desirous of wars, and [at different times] contrary to himself.[25]

It is in this connection that Irenaeus records Marcion's well-known attempt to set up a "New Testament" not in fulfilment of the Old, but in replacement of it and in contradiction to it. "He mutilated the Gospel According to Luke," we read,

> removing everything about the birth of the Lord, and much of the teaching of the words of the Lord, in which the Lord is recorded as clearly confessing the creator of this universe as his Father. . . . He also similarly cut up the Epistles of Paul, removing whatever the apostle said clearly about the God who made the world, that he is the Father of our Lord Jesus Christ, and whatever the apostle teaches by referring to the prophetic writings that predict the coming of the Lord.[26]

Whether by native genius or by divine inspiration, the Church responded to Marcion not negatively by rejecting his proposed canon of Scripture, but affirmatively by expanding it to include Christian writings that were obviously Jewish along with those materials which Marcion was trying to interpret as anti-Jewish. Thus it well may be said that because of the heretic Marcion the church first came to recognize a body of Christian Scriptures to be set beside the existing Jewish canon. In much the same way, and for just the same kind of reason, such assaults as Marcion's upon the God of the Jews may be thought to have stimulated and intensified the Church's positive teaching about that God as the true Father of the Saviour Jesus Christ.

The anonymous letter to Diognetus, dating from about A.D. 130, holds that before the coming of Jesus there was no real knowledge of God on the earth. "On the contrary," it says, "it was really the Ruler of all, the Creator of all, the invisible God himself, who from heaven established the truth and the holy, incomprehensible word among men." It is to be noted that here there is no explicit reference to the Old Testament revelation. Indeed the implication seems to be, despite mention of God as "the Master and Maker of the universe," that there had been no significant prior revelation at all.[27]

Fifty years later, in Athens, Athenagoras is perfectly willing to identify the God of Sophocles and Euripides with the God of the Christians. He quotes also, however, and manifestly he regards as much higher theological authority, both Exodus and Deutero-Isaiah. Adding in the doctrine of the Spirit, here with a supporting line from the book of Proverbs, he arrives at what can only be called an explicitly Trinitarian position:

to know the true God and his Word, to know the unity of the Father with the Son, the fellowship of the Father with the Son, what the Spirit is, what unity exists between these three, the Spirit, the Son, and the Father, and what is their distinction in unity.[28]

For Irenaeus it is clearly and only the God of Israel who is "the true God, who had established and made the whole human race." "There is one God Almighty," he insists, "who made all things by his Word, both visible and invisible." From the Fourth Gospel he cites the story of Nathanael, remarking that "the Israelite knew his King, in that he said to him, 'Rabbi, you are the Son of God, you are the King of Israel.'" Then, following St. Matthew, Irenaeus applies to Jesus the Deutero-Isaiah passage beginning, "Behold my beloved Son, in whom I am well pleased." Of the Gospels themselves he declares, "All of these handed down to us that there is one God, maker of heaven and earth, proclaimed by the Law and the Prophets, and one Christ the Son of God." [29]

Out of experience and its experimental recording, out of challenge and response, the Christian faith was moving into a formulation of its basic values and meanings. The Son of God was the Saviour. The Spirit of God was the vitalizing power. The will of a real, living, and eternal God was behind it all; and this eternal God, the Father of the Son, was none other than *JHVH* of Israel, the God of the Jewish faith.

These materials for the doctrine of the Trinity were available from the beginning of the Christian story. By the late second century they had become so clearly identified, each in its own right, that the next step inevitably was to try to determine how these realities of Christian experience fitted together in one coherent and ultimate Reality. The process of this unifying interpretation began no later than the writings of Paul. Its historic development from that point on will concern us next. The further continuing of the interpretive process will concern every thinking Christian always.

The Formulation

THE STORY of the interpretation in words, of what had been recognized in immediate experience, began with the New Testament. It started in truth with the new and living covenant of Christian faith even before any part of that covenant was expressed in writing. It continued, at an accelerating pace, through the first three Christian centuries. A principal milestone was the decision of the First Ecumenical Council, held at Nicea in the year 325.

That council marked however a single climax, and not at all a changeless conclusion. A second chapter in this section will therefore seek to follow the debates and determinations about the doctrine of the Trinity from the early fourth century to about the beginning of the tenth. Following this there will be attempted a survey of the further history down to our own time.

VII. THE ROAD TO NICEA

The most clearly Trinitarian statement in the King James version of the Bible is not an authentic part of Holy Scripture. That negative datum needs to be examined before we proceed to follow affirmative paths. As the passage stands in the traditional English text of the first epistle of St. John, it reads:

> For there are three that bear record in heaven, the Father, the Word, and the Holy Ghost: and these three are one. And there are three that bear witness in earth, the spirit, and the water, and the blood: and these three agree in one.[1]

This reading is supported by sixteenth century editions of the Latin Vulgate, but it did not appear in the early Latin translations, nor in their definitive revision by St. Jerome. It stands in no Greek manuscript earlier than 1520. It obviously was unknown to any of the early Fathers of the Church.

Erasmus of Rotterdam, not finding it in any of the manuscripts from which he was editing the first printed Greek New Testament, left it out of his first edition. It is said that, when challenged on the point by some traditionalists, he replied testily that he would include the disputed passage if they could produce a single Greek manuscript which showed it. Shortly afterwards they did: that of 1520, quite possibly manufactured for the purpose. True to his word, and against his better judgment, Erasmus added it in his third edition, published in 1522. Thence it passed into the "Received Text" of 1550, from which the King James version was made.

The original text, attested by all the principal manuscripts and by all but two of the more than five thousand lesser and later ones, is simply, "There are three who bear witness, the spirit and the water and the blood, and these three are at one." The expansion most probably began as a perfectly sincere interpretive comment, added marginally by a scribe or reader in the middle fourth century, and later mistakenly inserted into the text of some Latin copies of the epistle (though not of any Greek ones for more than eleven hundred years). It is first quoted by the Spanish Bishop Priscillian, whose career ended about A.D. 385.

In 1897, under Leo XIII, the Vatican declared the passage to be an integral part of the epistle. Accordingly it is included in the English translation issued by the Confraternity of Christian Doctrine in 1941. There is a footnote, however, conceding that the shorter form is supported by "the evidence of many manuscripts, and the majority of commentators." Four years before that, in the single-handed translation by the Dominican scholar Francis Aloysius Spencer, the footnote reads, "The majority of Catholic critics today hold that they were not part of the original text." [2]

The Revised Standard Version omits the Trinitarian reference without even offering a footnote, and so does the annotated edition of that version published by the Oxford University Press. This is true also of the Moffatt and Goodspeed renderings, and of the New English Bible. Members of the Disciples of Christ will be interested to know that this outcome of textual scholarship was anticipated as early as 1826 by Alexander Campbell, the founder of their denomination, in a translation of the New Testament which he sponsored and to which he contributed prefaces, emendations, and appendices. [3]

The case as to authenticity is not debatable: the Trinitarian sentence has to be rejected as an interpolation. The question of truth is not here at issue. Whether or not we accept the declaration as true, we may not regard it as a New Testament statement of doctrine. For anything of that character we must look elsewhere.

So far as we can tell, the earliest authentic verbal collocation of the three Persons of the Trinity is in the "Grace" which now stands at the end of II Corinthians: "The grace of the Lord Jesus Christ, and the love of God, and the communion of the Holy Ghost, be with you all." [4] This may be actually a part of the letter called "Corinthians C," and earlier than II Corinthians 1-9. In any event, it was the conclusion of one of Paul's letters to Corinth, and it would seem to reflect an attempt on his part to bring together basic values of the Christian faith and life. Nor is there any such variation in manuscript evidence as would cast doubt on the early date and the authenticity of this brief prayer.

At the same time, we have to recognize that this was far from being, or even from becoming, a standard formula for the apostle. He seems never to have returned to using it. The two "endings" of Romans are, respectively, "Now the God of peace be with you all," and "To God only wise, be glory through Jesus Christ for ever." Colossians has simply "Grace be with you," and Philemon "The grace of the Lord Jesus Christ be with your spirit." Thus also Philippians concludes, "The grace of our Lord Jesus Christ be with you all." [5]

Ephesians, Hebrews, the pastorals, and the so-called "general epistles," all of later dates than the authentic Pauline writings, are equally lacking in specifically Trinitarian expression. Ephesians prays for "Peace to the brethren, and love with faith, from God the Father and the Lord Jesus Christ." Hebrews has near its close a benediction which brings together "the God of peace" and "our Lord Jesus," but without mention of the Holy Spirit. I Timothy ends simply: "Grace be with thee," and Titus: "Grace be with you all." II Timothy concludes with "The Lord Jesus Christ be with thy [singular] spirit. Grace be with you [plural]." The two letters traditionally ascribed to Peter refer to "Christ Jesus" and to "our Lord and Saviour Jesus Christ" in their closing verses. Jude does seem to have something like a Trinitarian formula in "praying in the Holy Ghost, keep yourselves in the love of God, looking for the mercy of our Lord Jesus Christ unto eternal life." But immediately he moves on to an ascription which could have been totally Jewish:

> Now unto him that is able to keep you from falling, and to present you faultless before the presence of his glory with exceeding joy, to the only wise God our Saviour, be glory and majesty, dominion and power, both now and ever. Amen.[6]

That is to say, there is no indication that the apostolic Church made consistent use of a Trinitarian formula, or indeed that it thought at all consciously in Trinitarian terms as such.

It is possible to argue that there are Trinitarian implications in the magnificent eighth chapter of Paul's letter to the Romans. The three Persons are mentioned together in two closely related verses:

> . . . ye are not in the flesh, but in the Spirit, if so be that the Spirit of God dwell in you. Now if any man have not the Spirit of Christ, he is none of his . . .

and, similarly,

> . . . if the Spirit of him that raised up Jesus from the
> dead dwell in you, he that raised up Christ from the
> dead shall also quicken your mortal bodies by his Spirit
> that dwelleth in you.[7]

This chapter of St. Paul, however, scarcely is to be regarded as a lecture in systematic theology. It is simply,
and sufficiently, a soaring declaration of an experiential
faith. It illustrates again what we have noted often already:
that the materials for the construction of a systematic
doctrine of the Trinity were in the possession of the early
Church, and that they are clearly present in the New
Testament.

The only explicit juxtaposition of the three Persons
found in the canonical Gospels, and possibly but not certainly the first known listing of them in their now traditional order, stands at the close of the Gospel of St. Matthew. "Go ye therefore," says the risen Christ, "and teach
all nations, baptizing them in the name of the Father, and
of the Son, and of the Holy Ghost." [8] If this be an authentic saying of Jesus, it must mean that an essential Trinitarianism definitely was taught by our Lord himself, and
so that the disciples and the whole Church should have
known it, accepted, and taught it, from the beginning.

Apart from any dubiety as to the historical character of
the post-resurrection sayings attributed to Jesus, the evidence we have just been observing in the New Testament
literature shows that no such knowledge existed and that
no such acceptance and teaching had occurred. It is clear
also that the early baptismal practice did not include the

Trinitarian phrasing set forth in St. Matthew. The converts on the first Whitsunday were baptized simply "in the name of Jesus Christ." Those at Samaria "were baptized in the name of the Lord Jesus," as were those at Ephesus some two decades later.[9]

A slight presaging of a Trinitarian type of baptism is thought to be contained in Paul's "ye are washed . . . ye are sanctified . . . ye are justified in the name of the Lord Jesus, and by the Spirit of our God." There is no suggestion of this, however, in the preceding query in the same letter, "Is Christ divided? was Paul crucified for you? or were ye baptized in the name of Paul?" Nor is there in the still earlier, "as many of you as have been baptized into Christ have put on Christ." [10]

In all probability, the first actual appearance of the Trinitarian baptismal formula, and indeed of our standard Trinitarian phrasing at all, is that in the *Didache,* "The Teaching of the Twelve Apostles," a Syrian or Alexandrian church manual of about A.D. 110. "Baptize in running water," it instructs the readers,

> "in the name of the Father and of the Son and of the Holy Spirit." If you do not have running water, baptize in some other. If you cannot in cold, then in warm. If you have neither, then pour water on the head three times "in the name of the Father, Son, and Holy Spirit." [11]

Evidently the mode of baptism here is regarded as of secondary importance, and might be varied according to circumstance. The verbal formula, however, clearly is mandatory.

Many scholars are of the opinion that this passage in the *Didache* is prior to, and actually the source of, the one in St. Matthew. Even if it is not, the evidence is clear that our familiar triple phrasing was not employed in baptisms, nor regularly in any other connection in the Church, until about the beginning of the second century. Then, however, there began a process of rapid change.

By the middle of that century the triune formula had become a part of standard Christian usage. Justin's account of Christian worship reports that "they are then washed in the water in the name of God the Father and Master of all, and of our Saviour Jesus Christ, and of the Holy Spirit." Thirty years later Irenaeus waxes sarcastic about the elaborate baptismal formulae devised by the Gnostics, and obviously based upon the now orthodox one. "In the Name of the unknowable Father of all things—" runs one, "in Truth the mother of all—in him who came down upon Jesus—into union and redemption and the fellowship of the Powers." [12]

From the usage in baptism, the triple pattern of the Christian declaration of faith rapidly was extended into other connections. It seems to be the foundation for Justin's early adumbration of what became known as the *regula fidei,* the "rule of faith," and which developed ultimately into our Apostles' Creed. "It is Jesus Christ," Justin says,

> who has taught us these things, having been born for this purpose and crucified under Pontius Pilate, who was procurator of Judea in the time of Tiberius Caesar. We will show that we honor him in accordance with reason, having learned that he is the Son of the true God himself, and holding him to be in the second place and the prophetic Spirit in the third rank.[13]

70

There can be no doubt of the authority and the central importance of the Trinitarian concept for Athenagoras, who is defending the faith as the second century moves into its final quarter. He insists that God is one: "uncreated, eternal, invisible, impassible, incomprehensible, illimitable." Then, journeying comfortably with the Stoics and Philo, he proceeds,

> By him the Universe was created through his Word (*Logos*), was set in order, and is held together. [I say "his Word"], for we also think that God has a Son.
> Let no one think it stupid for me to say that God has a Son . . . the son of God is his Word in idea and in actuality; for by him and through him all things were made, the Father and the Son being one.

Immediately after this the Spirit is introduced:

> And since the Son is in the Father and the Father in the Son by the unity and power of the Spirit, the Son of God is the mind and Word of the Father.[14]

This Holy Spirit, "who inspires those who utter prophecies, is an effluence from God, flowing from him and returning to him like a ray of the sun." The conclusion of the matter is a ringing (even if ultimately not quite orthodox) Trinitarianism:

> Who, then, would not be astonished to hear those called atheists who admit God the Father, God the Son, and the Holy Spirit, and who teach their unity in power and their distinction in rank?

The Christians, Athenagoras insists further,

> are guided by this alone—to know the true God and his Word, to know the unity of the Father with the Son, the fellowship of the Father with the Son, what the Spirit is, what unity exists between these three, the Spirit, the Son, and the Father, and what is their distinction in unity.

And again,

> We speak of God, of the Son, his Word, and of the Holy
> Spirit; and we say that the Father, the Son, and the
> Spirit are united in power. For the Son is the intelli-
> gence, reason, and wisdom of the Father, and the Spirit
> is an effluence, as light from fire.[15]

Thus, a full century and a half before the convening
of the Nicene Council, the general structure is decisively
established. The word "Trinity" indeed has not yet appeared. The meaning nevertheless is here, waiting quietly
for the word which will sum it up.

Our word "Trinity" of course is Latin in origin (*trinitas*), and in this Latin form it appeared in Christian circles
before the equivalent Greek *trias* was ever applied to the
Godhead. Apparently we owe the theological use of
"Trinity" to the first great Christian writer in Latin, the
Carthaginian lawyer Tertullian. In his vigorous reply to
the "modalist" Praxeas, who evidently has been insisting
on the unitary nature of God, Tertullian writes:

> All are of One, by unity (that is) of substance; while
> the mystery of the dispensation is still guarded, which
> distributes the Unity into a Trinity, placing in their
> order the three Persons—the Father, the Son, and the
> Holy Ghost: three, however, not in condition, but in
> degree; not in substance, but in form; not in power, but
> in aspect; yet of one substance, and of one condition,
> and of one power, inasmuch as He is one God, from
> whom these degrees and forms and aspects are reckoned,
> under the name of the Father, and of the Son, and of
> the Holy Ghost.[16]

This refutation of Praxeas' views belongs to Tertullian's
Montanist period, but it reflects no peculiarly Montanist

positions. Almost universally it has been regarded as one of the sources of, and authorities for, the doctrine of the Trinity as ultimately it was phrased and accepted. Much earlier, and definitely in his pre-Montanist days, Tertullian had been no less emphatic about his position. He speaks of baptism as "the washing away of sin, which Faith obtaineth, being sealed in the Father, and in the Son, and in the Holy Ghost." And he concludes the argument by declaring that "where three are, that is, the Father and the Son and the Holy Ghost, there is the Church." [17]

St. Cyprian, Bishop of Carthage in the strenuous days from 248 or 249 to 258, contended vigorously for the unity of the Church, and against any concession either to the "lapsed" who had repudiated their Christian profession during the persecution by Decius, or to heretics of whatsoever sort. Cyprian associates the baptismal formula in St. Matthew directly with the word "Trinity." After quoting Jesus' reported saying, he continues, "He taught them that Trinity, in whose name the nations were to be baptized." In the same discussion of baptism he angrily rejects the earlier and simpler form of words:

> How can it be said that "wherever and however" a Gentile is baptized, outside the Church, "provided that it is in the name of Jesus Christ," he can obtain remission of sins, when Christ himself commands that the nations should be baptized in the full and united Trinity? [18]

"Trinity" is not the only word that needs defining, and by no means the only one that has created great problems in the process of definition. In the paragraph quoted above from Tertullian's reply to Praxeas we find "Persons" and "substance," neither of which terms presents a single and obvious denotation. The *persona* in Latin was not a discrete individual in the sense in which we use the word "person." It was specifically the mask worn by an actor in a play. Thus, in an extreme and not unattractive simplifying of the Trinitarian position, the three "Persons" of the Trinity were understood to be three several manifestations of the single deity: respectively as Creator, as Saviour, and as indwelling Power: but not at all as separately existing entities.

Tertullian's description of this view, as held by Praxeas, runs thus:

> The devil has striven against the truth in manifold ways. He has sometimes endeavored to destroy it by defending it. He champions the unity of God, the omnipotent creator of the world, only to make out of that unity a heresy. He says that the Father himself descended into the virgin, was himself born of her, himself suffered; in fact that he himself was Jesus Christ. . . . It was Praxeas who first brought this kind of perversity from Asia to Rome. . . . He put the Paraclete to flight and crucified the Father.[19]

The supposed crucifixion of the Father is referred to as "Patripassianism," the Father's suffering. At this date one wonders how far it has reappeared in the thinking of the "death of God" theologians.

Later in the third century this type of monistic, "modalist," or "monarchian" view of God became especially associated with the activities of one Sabellius, who went to Rome from Libya. According to Epiphanius of Salamis, writing of the still-persisting Sabellians a hundred years or so later,

Their doctrine is, that Father, Son and Holy Spirit are one and the same being, in the sense that three names are attached to one substance. A close analogy may be found in the body, soul, and spirit of man. The body is as it were the Father; the soul is the Son; while the Spirit is to the Godhead as his spirit is to a man. Or take the sun: it is one substance, but it has three manifestations, light, heat, and the orb itself.[20]

Sabellius and his associates duly were excommunicated. It was easier to condemn, however, than it was wholly to clarify. One principal difficulty from the beginnings, and a continuing one for us, is illustrated in the comparing of Tertullian's use of *substantia,* which we render naturally enough as "substance," with Epiphanius' treatment of the Greek *hypostasis,* also translated "substance" in the passage just quoted. The orthodox Tertullian insists on "one substance," and the orthodox Epiphanius condemns what sounds exactly like this position. How is this to be understood and explained?

Etymologically *substantia* and *hypostasis* would seem to be identical, being respectively under-standing and standing-under. Thus either or both might seem reasonably to be used to identify a basic groundwork, and so an essential unity. In usage, however, the two words moved in precisely opposite directions. The Latin *substantia* retained its native etymological force, as referring to a single and ultimate reality: therefore Tertullian's holding to "one substance." The Greek *hypostasis* carries exactly this meaning in the opening of the letter to the Hebrews, where "the express image of his person" actually is "the *character* of his *hypostasis.*" The Revised Standard's "the very stamp of his nature," and the New English "the stamp of God's very being," both indicate the essential reference to the divine essence.[21]

Ere long, however, this content was taken over by the word *ousia,* derived from a participial form of the Greek verb "to be." *Hypostasis* meanwhile definitely changed in character. I am indebted to one of my (several) favorite Greek restaurateurs for a modern light on this issue. I wrote down *hypostasis* in Greek characters, and handed over the slip of paper with a remark about "under-standing." He said immediately, "Yes, but we don't use it that way. With us it means 'difference,' or 'separation.'" This gentleman is not a trained theologian, but he is a legitimate inheritor of his own Eastern Church tradition. Well before the end of the third century, the East had come to use *hypostasis* in the plural, and so to identify three *hypostases* of one *ousia,* very much as the West was holding to three *personae* of one *substantia.*

It was in vain, and not with strict accuracy, that St. Jerome in the late fourth century argued to Pope Damasus that "in the whole range of secular learning *hypostasis* never means anything but *ousia.*"[22] Tempting as it may be to cut through all the arguments with the knife of modalism, and so to identify the Persons of the Trinity simply as three occasional manifestations of one Deity, each partial and none separate, we have to admit that neither in the East nor in the West did the orthodox Church accede to any such position. *Hypostasis* had ceased to mean essence, and *persona* had come to signify more than mask.

With the recognizing of this extent of differentiation in the Godhead, other problems immediately presented themselves. What precisely was the nature of the relation among the *hypostases?* The critical issue before Nicea was that of the relation of the Father to the Son. "A Father makes a Son, and a Son makes a Father," Tertullian had said to Praxeas.[23] This however was merely a matter of "making" by identification. Was the Son actually begotten of the Father? And had he been begotten at a point of time?

Origen poses the whole question of identity and distinction to Heraclides:

> Is it true then that there was a God, the Son of God, the only begotten of God, the firstborn of all creation, and that we need have no fear of saying that in one sense there are two Gods, while in another there is one God?

He offers his own reply, to the effect that

> in relation to the Father and God of the universe, our Saviour and Lord is not one flesh, nor one spirit, but something higher than flesh and spirit, namely, one God. The appropriate word when human beings are joined to one another is flesh. The appropriate word when a righteous man is joined to Christ is spirit. But the word when Christ is united to the Father is not flesh, nor spirit, but more honorable than these—God.

In practical application, then,

> When we pray, because of the one party let us preserve the duality, because of the other party let us hold to the unity. In this way we avoid falling into the opinion of those who have been separated from the Church and turned to the illusory notion of monarchy, who abolish the Son as distinct from the Father and virtually abolish

the Father also. Nor do we fall into the other blasphemous doctrine which denies the deity of Christ.[24]

This duality in unity, and unity in duality, completely failed to satisfy Arius, a presbyter in Alexandria early in the fourth century. The fifth-century historian Socrates vividly records Arius' appearance in the arena of theological dispute. "On one occasion," he tells us,

> at a gathering of his presbyters and the rest of the clergy, [Bishop Alexander of Alexandria] essayed a rather ambitious theological disquisition on the Holy Trinity, a metaphysical explanation of the Unity in Trinity. But one of the presbyters of his diocese, Arius by name, a man not lacking in dialectic, thinking that the bishop was expounding the doctrine of Sabellius the Libyan, from love of controversy espoused a view diametrically opposed to the teaching of the Libyan, and attacked the statements of the bishop with energy. "If," said he, "the Father begat the Son, he that was begotten had a beginning of existence; hence it is clear that there was [a time] when the Son was not. It follows then of necessity that he had his existence from the non-existent." [25]

In 318 Arius wrote to his former fellow student Eusebius, now Bishop of Nicomedia, protesting the views of Alexander. He quotes him as using the expressions, "Always Father, always Son," "The Son exists unbegottenly with God," "The Son is of God himself," etc. This Arius seems to have regarded as unabashed Sabellianism. His own position, in contrast, was

> that the Son is not unbegotten, nor a part of the unbegotten in any way . . . but that he was constituted by [God's] will and counsel, before times and before ages, full (of grace and truth), divine, unique, unchangeable.

And before he was begotten or created or ordained or founded, he was not.[26]

To Bishop Alexander himself Arius and thirteen of his associates addressed a manifesto, probably in an attempt to prevent the excommunication which nevertheless occurred in 321. After joining with all the orthodox in assailing the Gnostics, the Manicheans, and the Sabellians, this set forth that

> . . . there are three *hypostases*. God being the cause of all things is without beginning and most unique, while the Son, begotten timelessly by the Father and created before ages and established, was not before he was begotten—but, begotten timelessly before all things, he alone was constituted by the Father. He is neither eternal nor co-eternal nor co-unbegotten with the Father. . . . God is thus before all. Therefore he is also prior to the Son.[27]

Arius nonetheless was excommunicated in Alexandria. In Asia Minor two years later he was recognized as being orthodox. The resulting extension of the controversy, and its increasing heat, led the newly converted Emperor Constantine I to call for a meeting of the Bishops of the Church in formal Council. The gathering convened in Nicea, in northwestern Asia Minor across the Bosphorus from what was to become the Emperor's new capital of Constantinople. Only four Bishops from the West were present. One of these, however, was Hosius of Cordova in Spain, Constantine's personal religious adviser; and it was he who became the presiding officer.

Eusebius, Bishop of Caesarea, was of those who had given Arius sanctuary after the conflict in Alexandria. For this, and for allegedly holding to Arian views, he had been condemned by a synod meeting at Antioch. At the opening of the Nicene Council, apparently, Eusebius was called upon to explain his views, and to defend his status as an orthodox believer. His attempt to do so is embodied in this formula, as he himself reports it:

> We believe in one God, Father, Almighty, the maker of all things visible and invisible,
>
> And in one Lord Jesus Christ, the Word of God, God of god, Light of Light, Life of Life, unique Son, first-born of all creation, begotten of the Father before all the ages, through whom also all things came to be, who for our salvation was incarnate and dwelt among men and suffered and rose on the third day and ascended to the Father and will come again with glory to judge living and dead.
>
> We also believe in one Holy Spirit.

"Believing that each of these is and exists," Eusebius continued,

> The Father truly Father, the Son truly Son, and the Holy Spirit truly Holy Spirit, as also our Lord said when sending forth his disciples . . . of which I firmly assert that this is what I hold, and so I am convinced, and so I have held, and will stand for this faith till death, anathematizing every godless heresy.
>
> That I have always been convinced of these things, heart and soul, since I was first conscious of myself, and so I am now convinced and profess—[this] I witness in truth before God Almighty and our Lord Jesus Christ, and am prepared to demonstrate and prove to you that so I believed and preached in times gone by.[28]

This was all right so far as it went, but for Hosius at least it did not go far enough. The tradition that Athanasius was the principal defender of Trinitarian orthodoxy (as we have come to know it) at the Nicene Council is not to be credited. At this time he was only thirty years old, a mere deacon in the Alexandrian church, and thus junior to Arius. He was secretary to his Bishop, and apparently served as his theological adviser. He was not, and could not have been, a major figure in the Council's formal discussions.

Eusebius' account is that the Emperor himself, though favorably impressed by the formula as presented, urged the adding of the word *homoousios,* "consubstantial," "of the same essence." If indeed it was Constantine who suggested this, it surely must have been at the instance of his adviser Hosius. Eusebius' statement may have served as a basis for the Council's own declaration, but it was expanded and altered in order to achieve a flat denial of Arian views:

> We believe in one God, Father, Almighty, maker of all things, visible and invisible,
> And in one Lord Jesus Christ, begotten of the Father uniquely, that is, of the substance of the Father, God of God, Light of Light, true God of true God, begotten, not made, consubstantial (*homoousion*) with the Father, through whom all things were made, both things in heaven and those in earth, who for us men and for our salvation came down and was incarnate, [and] became man; he suffered and rose on the third day, ascended into heaven, and is coming to judge living and dead,
> And in the Holy Spirit.
> But those who say, there was once when he was not, and before he was begotten he was not and he came into being out of things that are not, or allege that the Son of God is of different subsistence or essence, or created

or alterable or changeable, the catholic and apostolic Church anathematizes.[29]

For the time being, Eusebius rationalized himself into accepting these changes. "I agreed to this idea," he says, "not rejecting the word *homoousios,* having before me the aim of peace, and that of not falling away from the sound doctrine." It is hard to credit his ingenuousness when he continues, "Nor did I think it improper to anathematize the term, 'Before he was begotten he was not,' since all confess that the Son of God was before [his] generation according to the flesh." [30] Obviously the "generation according to the flesh" was not at all the point at issue; and so the Bishop's dodging of the issue is obvious too.

Nevertheless he was restored to good standing among his fellows, and held his see for another fifteen years, till his death in 340. This is not to say that he was even ostensibly an upholder of strict Nicene orthodoxy throughout that time. But the details of the post-Nicene controversies must await attention in the next chapter.

It is impossible fully to assess the rights and the wrongs, the gains and the losses, in the Nicene settlement. What does seem to be clear is that an acceptance of the Arian position, with reference to the subordination of the Son, would have issued almost inevitably in a pluralism, if not an actual polytheism, in the Christian doctrine of deity. Once the Redeemer was separated from God the Father and seen as in any way inferior to him, the natural consequence would have been the development (as with the Gnostics earlier) of an increasingly numerous series of mediating emanations between God and man. The result of this, in turn, scarcely could have been other than the dissipation of Christian allegiance into a galloping sectarianism.

The acceptance of the *homoousios,* on the other hand, with its insistence upon the real unity of the Son with the Father, guaranteed the absolute primacy of the Godhead over all other beings whatsoever. Difficult as the Creed of Nicea may be to comprehend, it is undeniably a declaration of the divine oneness. As such it allowed no room for scattering and divided loyalties among believers; and so it provided, in a way that Arianism never could have offered, a continuing foundation for the oneness of the Church itself.

VIII. DISPUTINGS AND DEFININGS

Only a few Christian believers of today, even among those who say the "Nicene Creed" regularly in their church services, ever have realized that the formula they recite is one which differs substantially from that approved in 325 at Nicea. As has been said, the Nicene Council marked a climax in the history of Christian dogma. It is also true that it was followed by controversies even more furious than those which had preceded it.

Athanasius contra mundum, "Athanasius against the world," is a phrase which belongs not to the Council itself but to the period after it. This most famous protagonist of Trinitarian orthodoxy became the patriarch of Alexandria in 328, and he died there in 373. In between, however, he was deposed and exiled five different times: the first in 335 under Constantine "the Great," the fourth in 362 under Julian "the Apostate," and the fifth in 365 under the Arian Emperor Valens.

That Julian and Valens scarcely were orthodox Christians is obvious enough. Some question arises, however, as to the orthodoxy of the "first Christian Emperor," the imperial patron of the Nicene decree. The answer has to be that Constantine's loyalty to that settlement was both superficial and temporary. What he wanted was peace in the Church, for the sake of the Empire. With Hosius at the other end of the Mediterranean, the pressure (from 330 on) of the semi-Arian Eastern bishops steadily moved the theologically illiterate ruler away from the position he had thought to take.

On Constantine's death in 337 the Eastern and Western empires were divided, with Constans I ruling in Rome and Constantius II in Byzantium. Constans died in 350, and Constantius made himself sole Emperor in 351. He was openly, and it seems honestly, an Arian Christian. He did allow Athanasius to resume his see after Constantine had died, but forced him out again in 339, two years later.

Athanasius fled to Rome, where he found himself supported by Pope Julius I. That pontiff urged the bishops of the East to restore their former colleague. Instead of doing this, ninety of them, meeting at Antioch in 341 for the dedication of Constantine's "Golden Church," set forth a creed which was so strongly anti-Sabellian that it was unmistakably Arian. "A Father who is truly Father," it said,

a Son who is truly Son and a Holy Spirit who is truly

Holy Spirit, the titles not being given in a vague or meaningless way but accurately denoting the particular existence (*hypostasis*) and rank and glory of each that is so named, so that they are three in existence (*hypostasis*) but one in agreement.

Appended to this was a statement which sounded anti-Arian, but was not. "If any one teaches," these bishops declared, ". . . that there was a time or season or age before the begetting of the Son of God, let him be anathema." [1] But Arius had carefully avoided saying anything about time in this connection. His formula, carefully thought through and very carefully phrased, had been only "there was when he was not." That, of course—all time considerations apart —was decisive as to the secondary "rank and glory" of the Son.

Meeting at Sardica (the modern Sofia) in 343, the Western bishops replied with a resounding endorsement at once of Athanasius and of the Creed of Nicea. In 346, apparently to show a semblance of harmony with the Western Constans, Constantius once more permitted Athanasius to return to Alexandria. During a decade of relative peace there, the reinstated patriarch wrote his most notable work, the *Defence Against the Arians.* Constantius left him undisturbed for the first five years of his sole imperial rule, but drove him out again in 356.

At a council at Sirmium in the Western Balkans the next year, the Arians proved to be in complete control. "Many are disturbed," they said,

by questions about "substance" (*substantia*), or in Greek *ousia,* that is, to make it more clearly understood, about the term *homoousion* [of the same substance], or the phrase *homoiousion* [of like substance]. Therefore no mention ought to be made of these, nor any exposition of them in the church; for this reason, that they are not contained in the divine Scriptures and because they are beyond the understanding of man . . .

There is no doubt [they continued] that the Father is greater . . . than the Son in honour, renown, and deity . . . And every one knows that this is catholic doctrine, that there are two persons of the Father and the Son; and that the Father is greater, the Son subject together with all the things that the Father has subjected to himself. That the Father has not a beginning, is invisible, immortal, and impassible; that the Son has been born from the Father.[2]

Hilary of Poitiers, who substantially had taken the place of Hosius as the Western spokesman for Nicene orthodoxy, referred to this document as "the blasphemy of Sirmium." From Sirmium two years later there came a more moderate, and so presumably less blasphemous, declaration. This, too, sought to outlaw the *homoousion,* "same substance," but it did so by indirection:

But the term "essence" (*ousia*) had been taken up by the Fathers rather unwisely, and gives offence because it is not understood by the people. It is also not contained in the Scriptures. For these reasons we have decided to do away with it, and that no use at all shall be made of it for the future in connection with God, because the divine Scriptures nowhere use it of the Father and the Son. But we say that the Son is like the Father in all things, as the holy Scriptures say and teach.[3]

This swing of the pendulum pleased the Arian Emperor not at all. He called the Western bishops to Aruminum, and the Eastern ones to Seleucia, to devise a restatement.

Both groups were disposed to be recalcitrant, but both were beaten down. At last at Constantinople, in 360, a Council approved a joint product as it was demanded by the Emperor. This added a taboo on the word *hypostasis* to that on *ousia,* and reduced "like the Father in all things" to simply "like the Father." "The world groaned and marveled at finding itself Arian," commented the Western and orthodox Jerome.[4]

This Creed of early 360 nevertheless was the one which Ulfilas, the first missionary to the Goths, took with him and taught to his converts for another twenty years. It was maintained in many of the Germanic churches for three centuries more. Elsewhere, however, it was quickly superseded and forgotten.

Constantius died in 361. The resilient Athanasius returned promptly from his third exile, and despite the two brief interruptions under the Emperors Julian and Valens respectively, pursued his warfare for the orthodox position. Ably assisted in the West by Hilary, up to that worthy's death in 367, and increasingly in the East by Basil the Great of Caesarea, he gained with them a posthumous but thorough triumph in the Council of Constantinople in 381.

Traditionally it was at this Council, the second of those unanimously recognized as ecumenical although it was made up only of bishops of the East, that the "Nicene Creed" took the form in which we know it. This may be in substance true. The actual documents produced, however, have not been preserved, or at least have not been discovered to date. The existing contemporary evidence is in a letter from the Eastern bishops to some Western ones, declining an invitation to a proposed Council in Rome but assuring them of full agreement in Nicene orthodoxy. "We withstood all," they say,

> for the sake of the gospel faith as authenticated by the 318 fathers at Nicea . . . it . . . teaches us to believe in the name of the Father and of the Son and of the Holy Spirit . . . in one Godhead and power and substance . . . of equal dignity and coeternal majesty, in three perfect *hypostases.* . . .
>
> Thus no place is found for the error of Sabellius in which the *hypostases* are confused and their individualities taken away . . . nor does the blasphemy of the . . . Arians . . . prevail, in which the substance, or nature of the God is cut up and some kind of later nature, created and of a different substance, is added to the uncreated and consubstantial and coeternal Trinity.

Of the incarnate Lord these bishops testified "that he existed as perfect God, the Word, before all ages, and became perfect man in the last days for our salvation." [5]

It was at Chalcedon, a full seventy years later, that the "Nicene Creed" received what must be regarded as its first certainly official statement. The text there set forth, and explicitly identified as the one written in 381 at Constantinople, is that still used in Eastern Orthodoxy:

> We believe in one God, Father Almighty, maker of heaven and earth, and of all things visible and invisible, And in one Lord Jesus Christ, the unique Son of God, begotten of the Father before all the ages, Light of Light, true God of true God, begotten, not made, through whom all things came into being; who for us men and for our salvation came down from heaven, and was incarnate of [the] Holy Spirit and Mary the Virgin, and became man; he was crucified also for us under Pontius

Pilate, and suffered, and was buried, and rose again on the third day according to the Scriptures; and ascended into heaven, and sits on the right hand of the Father, and is coming again with glory to judge living and dead; of whose Kingdom there will be no end.

And in the Holy Spirit, the Lord, and the Life-giver, who proceeds from the Father, who with the Father and the Son is worshiped and glorified, who spoke through the prophets—[and] in one Holy Catholic and Apostolic Church; we confess one Baptism for the remission of sins. We look for the resurrection of the dead, and the life of the age to come. Amen.[6]

It will be seen that the differences from the familiar Western form are slight. Only one of them is theologically important. The West restored the Nicene "God of God" before "Light of Light," and apparently Archbishop Thomas Cranmer inadvertently omitted the word "Holy" before "Catholic and Apostolic Church." The single significant Western departure from the formula of Chalcedon is the addition of the famous *filioque,* which gives the reading "who proceedeth from the Father and the Son."

This, however, must be set aside for later discussion. The Chalcedonian decree itself reflects earlier controversies. It demands therefore that now we look somewhat more closely at the thinking, and the discussions and disputes, of some of the principal theologians of the late fourth and early fifth centuries.

From the attempt to analyze and to define the precise interrelationships of the Persons of the Trinity, and so as it were to diagram the structure of the Godhead, enquiring theological thought had pressed on to raise the question as to the inner nature of the Second Person himself. Just in what senses was the Son God, and in what (if any) was he man?

One straightforward and apparently simple answer was that made by Apollinaris, Bishop of Laodicea in Syria in the late fourth century. It was to the effect that the Son had no human consciousness at all, but that "the Godhead of the only-begotten fulfills the function of mind." Thus the *Logos* did not "become flesh," but simply sojourned in the body of the Son of Man. One consequence of this view, as Gregory of Nazianzus pointed out in a letter written after the Chalcedon Council, was a recrudescence of Patripassianism: "His Godhead also was put to death with his body, and thus was raised again from the dead by the Father." [7]

"Do not let the men deceive themselves and others," Gregory warned his *locum tenens* Cledonius,

with the assertion that the "Man of the Lord," as they call him, who is rather our Lord and God, is without human mind. For we do not sever the man from the Godhead, but we lay down as a dogma the unity and identity [of person], who of old was not man but God, and the only Son before all ages, unmingled with body or anything corporeal; but who in these last days has assumed manhood also for our salvation; passible in his flesh, impassible in his Godhead; circumscript in the body, uncircumscript in the Spirit; at once earthly and heavenly, tangible and intangible, comprehensible and incomprehensible; that by one and the same [Person], who was perfect man and also God, the entire humanity fallen through sin might be created anew.[8]

The bishops meeting at Constantinople in 381 had repudiated the Apollinarian view, declaring that

> We also preserve unperverted the doctrine of the incarnation of the Lord, receiving the dispensation of the flesh as neither without soul nor without mind nor incomplete, but knowing that he existed as perfect God, the Word, before all ages, and became perfect man in the last days for our salvation.[9]

So much for the attempt to deny the genuine human nature of the Lord. A contrary trend was followed by Nestorius, who was Bishop of Constantinople from 428 to 431. Apparently in an effort completely to repudiate the Apollinarian heresy, Nestorius went to the other extreme of denying that the Virgin had given birth at all to the divine nature in Christ; and therefore that, as the mother of his humanity only, she ought never to be called *theotokos,* "Mother of God."

Defending his position in a letter to Celestine of Rome, Nestorius assailed those who "refer the Godhead of the Only-begotten to the same origin as the flesh joined [with it], and kill it with the flesh." Thus he was flatly and orthodoxly repudiating Apollinarianism. But he went on,

> They even dare to treat of the Christ-bearing Virgin in a way as along with God, for they do not scruple to call her *theotokos,* when the holy and beyond-all-praise Fathers at Nicea said no more of the holy Virgin than that our Lord Jesus Christ was incarnate of the Holy Spirit and the Virgin Mary—not to mention the Scriptures, which everywhere, both by angels and apostles, speak of the Virgin as mother of Christ, not of God the Word.[10]

Cyril, Bishop of Alexandria for a full generation, from 412 to 444, responded vigorously and even violently. "We must not separate the one Lord Christ into two Sons," he wrote to Nestorius early in the year 430. "He was born of a woman; but he did not cast aside his being God and his having been begotten of God the Father. He assumed our flesh; but he continued to be what he was." [11] This letter of Cyril was approved by a Council at Ephesus in 431, as was also an even more heated one written in the autumn of 430. This included a dozen anathemas, beginning with an assertion of the *theotokos,* and ending with one which insisted on the reality of the suffering of the Word of God in the flesh.[12] The earlier of these letters was specifically used as a criterion of orthodoxy at Chalcedon, but the later one was left unmentioned.

In 433 a partial reconciliation was effected between the Antiochene and Alexandrian views. "That the division which arose between the Churches was entirely superfluous and unjustified," Cyril wrote to Nestorius' successor John, "we are now thoroughly convinced." Paul, Bishop of Emesa, had worked out a document which Cyril quoted in full. "We confess, then," it said,

> our Lord Jesus Christ, the unique Son of God, perfect God and perfect man, of a reasonable soul and body; begotten of the Father before [the] ages according to the Godhead, the same in the last days for us and for our salvation [born] of Mary the Virgin according to the manhood; the same consubstantial with the Father in Godhead, and consubstantial with us in manhood, for a union of two natures took place; therefore we confess one Christ, one Son, one Lord.

"According to this understanding of the unconfused union," Bishop Paul had conceded, "we confess the holy Virgin to be *theotokos,* because God the Word was made flesh and lived as man, and from the very conception united to himself the temple taken from her." [13]

The truce was an uneasy one. After the death of Cyril in 444, the most vocal objector to the doctrine of the two natures turned out to be an elderly monk in Constantinople, named Eutyches. Charged with heresy in 448, he responded,

> I admit that our Lord was of two natures before the union, but after the union one nature. . . I follow the doctrine of the blessed Cyril and the holy fathers and the holy Athanasius. They speak of two natures before the union, but after the union and incarnation they speak of one nature, not two.[14]

What follows is not a pretty story. Eutyches was condemned at Constantinople, but then was upheld by Dioscorus, Cyril's successor at Alexandria, in the disorderly "Robber Synod" at Ephesus in 449. It was in reaction to these events, and after the death of the Emperor Theodosius II, that the Council of Chalcedon was convened.

In June of 449 Pope Leo I wrote from Rome to Flavian, patriarch of Constantinople. "While the distinctness of both natures and substances is preserved," he said, "and both meet in one Person, lowliness is assumed by majesty, weakness by power, mortality by eternity." "As the Word does not withdraw from equality with the Father in glory," the letter continued,

> so the flesh does not abandon the nature of our kind. For, as we must often be saying, he is one and the same, truly Son of God, and truly Son of Man: God, inasmuch as "in the beginning was the Word, and the Word was with God, and the Word was God"; Man, inasmuch as "the Word was made flesh, and dwelt among us." God, inas-

much as "all things were made by him, and without him nothing was made"; Man, inasmuch as he was "made of a woman, made under the law." [15]

This roundly and soundly Scriptural declaration, paradoxical as it was and continues to be, was specifically endorsed at Chalcedon, along with the first two letters of Cyril. The decree included also a clear quotation from the compromise formula of 433. "Following therefore the holy Fathers," said the bishops at Chalcedon,

> we confess one and the same our Lord Jesus Christ, and we all teach harmoniously [that he is] the same perfect in Godhead, the same perfect in manhood, truly God and truly man, the same of a reasonable soul and body; consubstantial (*homoousios*) with the Father in Godhead, and the same consubstantial with us in manhood, like us in all things except sin.

Mary was specifically designated as *theotokos,* and the two natures in Christ were said to combine "in one person and hypostasis." [16]

Chalcedon marked the definitive settlement of doctrine about the Person of Christ. Resistance persisted in many quarters, expressing itself in what became known as "monophysitism," the insistence on one nature only instead of two. As in the case of Arianism, imperial interferences and fluctuations complicated the matter. Ultimately the Coptic, Armenian, Abyssinian, and Syrian Jacobite Churches became definitely monophysite in doctrine, and therefore were repudiated as heretical by both the Catholic West and the Orthodox East. The main stream of Christianity was to flow hereafter in the channel charted at Chalcedon.

Attention had been directed by this time also to the doctrine of the Holy Spirit. The preliminary draft which Eusebius had offered at Nicea, and the final document approved by that Council, had limited reference simply to "We also believe in one Holy Spirit" and the even briefer "And in the Holy Spirit." Presumably at Constantinople in 381, and certainly at Chalcedon in 451, this was expanded into the form familiar to us:

> And in the Holy Spirit, the Lord, and the Life-giver, who proceeds from the Father, who with the Father and the Son is worshiped and glorified, who spoke through the prophets . . .[17]

The motive for the addition presumably was to make it clear that the Third Person of the Trinity, who had been largely neglected during the disputes about the Second Person, nevertheless merited serious attention. At the time there was nothing obviously controversial in the phrasing. "Who proceeds from the Father," which later was to become a subject of conflict and a major factor in the separation of the East and the West, was simply a quotation from the Fourth Gospel's account of Jesus' last discourse: "The Spirit of truth, which proceedeth from the Father." [18]

Almost casually, it would seem, a council at Toledo in 589 added to this the expression *filioque,* "and from the Son." Designed to emphasize the rejection of Arianism, this addition became generally popular in the West. Pope Leo in 809 refused to include it in the Creed, but under the influence of Charlemagne the practice continued outside Rome and in the course of time was quietly accepted there. In 867 Photius of Constantinople excommunicated Nicholas I of Rome for "corrupting the Creed" by this inclusion. To this day this is the only significant difference between the Creeds of the West and the East.

It was largely in the East that the Christological controversies were carried on, and it was principally there that the formal settlements were reached. Meanwhile, however, significant contributions to Trinitarian thinking were being made farther west along the Mediterranean. "To understand that Trinity soberly and piously," wrote St. Augustine before he became Bishop of Hippo, "occupies all the watchful care of Christians." This watchful care he exercised some twenty years later in his classic work *On the Trinity*.

Augustine made use of psychological categories to illustrate, if not wholly to define, the nature of the triune Godhead. "Here then," he wrote,

> is a kind of image of the Trinity: the mind itself, its knowledge which is at once its offspring and self-derived "word," and thirdly love. These three are one, and one single substance. The mind is no greater than its offspring, when its self-knowledge is equal to its being; nor than its love, when its self-love is equal to its knowledge and to its being.

He identified also a "triad of memory, understanding, and will . . . not three lives, but one; nor three minds, but one. It follows that they are not three substances, but one substance."

Already this Western thinker was pointing, and effectively, toward expression and acceptance of the *filioque*. "The Holy Spirit does not proceed from the Father into the Son, and then from the Son to sanctify the creature," he argued. "He proceeds at once from both." This was part of a sermon he had preached previously to his own congregation, and which now he quoted *verbatim* in the closing section of his extended theological analysis.[19]

In *The City of God* Augustine set forth a formal, if not altogether convincing, repudiation of Sabellianism:

> We do not say, as the Sabellian heretics say, that the Father is the same as the Son, and the Holy Spirit the same as the Father and the Son; but we say that the Father is the Father of the Son, and the Son the Son of the Father, and the Holy Spirit of the Father and the Son is neither the Father nor the Son.

Yet in the next book of the same work we read that while

> this whole is a Trinity by reason of the individuality [*proprietas*] of the persons, and one God by reason of the indivisible omnipotence; yet so that, when we inquire regarding each singly, it is said that each is God and Almighty; and, when we speak of all together, it is said that there are not three Gods, nor three Almighties, but one God Almighty: so great is the indivisible unity of these Three, which requires that it be so stated.

This indeed is not Sabellian. It seems rather to set forth a frankly monarchical view of the Deity.[20]

In the same tenor, and long before, Augustine had urged that "if we understand the changeless supereminence of the divine Being above every changeable thing, then Father, Son, and Holy Spirit 'moved over the waters.'" "Whether there is a Trinity there," he then wrote with reference to the being-knowing-willing analysis,

> because these three functions exist in the one God, or whether all three are in each Person so that they are each threefold, or whether both these notions are true, and in

97

some mysterious manner, the Infinite is in itself its own Selfsame object—at once one and many, so that by itself it is and knows itself without change, so that the Selfsame is the abundant magnitude of its Unity—who can readily conceive?

Thus he was able to speak, perhaps "in some mysterious manner" but certainly without embarrassment, of "the trinity of the Unity and the unity of the Trinity." [21]

It seems likely that the so-called "Athanasian Creed," the *Quicunque vult,* actually was an attempt to restate Nicene doctrine in terms of Augustine's analyses. This quasi-ecumenical document originated in Southern Gaul in the sixth century. Under Charlemagne it began to be used as a canticle, and was included in the monastic office of Prime. In the Church of England it still is required to be said or sung at Morning Prayer, instead of the Apostles' Creed, on thirteen major feast days. Officially accepted by the Lutheran bodies, it has dropped out of use in recent years, and it is not included in the new *Service Book and Hymnal* of the Lutheran Church in America.

Because the full text appears to be relatively inaccessible for most American readers, I reproduce it here:[22]

> Whosoever will be saved: before all things it is necessary that he hold the Catholick Faith.
> Which Faith except every one do keep whole and undefiled: without doubt he shall perish everlastingly.
> And the Catholick Faith is this: That we worship one God in Trinity, and Trinity in Unity;
> Neither confounding the Persons: nor dividing the Substance.
> For there is one Person of the Father, another of the Son: and another of the Holy Ghost.

But the Godhead of the Father, of the Son, and of the Holy Ghost, is all one: the Glory equal, the Majesty co-eternal.

Such as the Father is, such is the Son: and such is the Holy Ghost.

The Father uncreate, the Son uncreate: and the Holy Ghost uncreate.

The Father incomprehensible, the Son incomprehensible: and the Holy Ghost incomprehensible.

The Father eternal, the Son eternal: and the Holy Ghost eternal.

And yet they are not three eternals: but one eternal.

As also there are not three incomprehensibles, nor three uncreated: but one uncreated, and one incomprehensible.

So likewise the Father is Almighty, the Son Almighty: and the Holy Ghost Almighty.

And yet they are not three Almighties: but one Almighty.

So the Father is God, the Son is God: and the Holy Ghost is God.

And yet they are not three Gods: but one God.

So likewise the Father is Lord, the Son Lord: and the Holy Ghost Lord.

And yet not three Lords: but one Lord.

For like as we are compelled by the Christian verity: to acknowledge every Person by himself to be God and Lord;

So are we forbidden by the Catholick Religion: to say, There be three Gods, or three Lords.

The Father is made of none: neither created, nor begotten.

The Son is of the Father alone: not made, nor created, but begotten.

The Holy Ghost is of the Father and of the Son: neither made, nor created, nor begotten, but proceeding.

So there is one Father, not three Fathers; one Son, not three Sons: one Holy Ghost, not three Holy Ghosts.

And in this Trinity none is afore, or after other: none is greater, or less than another;

But the whole three Persons are co-eternal together: and co-equal.

So that in all things, as is aforesaid: the Unity in Trinity, and the Trinity in Unity is to be worshipped.

He therefore that will be saved: must thus think of the Trinity.

Futhermore, it is necessary to everlasting salvation: that he also believe rightly the Incarnation of our Lord Jesus Christ.

For the right Faith is, that we believe and confess: that our Lord Jesus Christ, the Son of God, is God and Man; God, of the substance of the Father, begotten before the worlds: and Man, of the Substance of his Mother, born in the world;

Perfect God, and perfect Man: of a reasonable soul and human flesh subsisting;

Equal to the Father, as touching his Godhead: and inferior to the Father, as touching his Manhood.

Who although he be God and Man: yet he is not two, but one Christ;

One; not by conversion of the Godhead into flesh: but by taking of the Manhood into God;

One altogether; not by confusion of Substance: but by unity of Person.

For as the reasonable soul and flesh is one man: so God and Man is one Christ;

Who suffered for our salvation: descended into hell, rose again the third day from the dead.

He ascended into heaven, he sitteth on the right hand of the Father, God Almighty: from whence he shall come to judge the quick and the dead.

At whose coming all men shall rise again with their bodies: and shall give account for their own works.

And they that have done good shall go into life ever-lasting: and they that have done evil into everlasting fire.

This is the Catholick Faith: which except a man believe faithfully, he cannot be saved.

Glory be to the Father, and to the Son: and to the Holy Ghost;

As it was in the beginning, is now, and ever shall be: world without end. Amen.

It is not difficult to see why in our time the *Quicunque vult* has slipped into desuetude. Its length and repetitiousness are against it, to begin with. The "Proposed" English Prayer Book of 1928, which the House of Commons refused to approve, would have made its use wholly voluntary, and suggested the using of one half or the other at different seasons.

Naturally enough, the reference to "the Father incomprehensible, the Son incomprehensible: and the Holy Ghost incomprehensible," has encouraged sardonic remarks to the effect that the whole thing (whether the Creed or the doctrine) is incomprehensible. More serious is the criticism that this formula seeks to make theological conformity a *sine qua non* of salvation. It is interesting to note that the English revisers, in indicating partial uses, left out both the opening and the closing demands for full agreement.

Affirmatively, we ought to note the specific defences of orthodox Christian thought which the *Quicunque vult* was trying to make. The former parts are obviously Nicene and Chalcedonian, with Augustinian overtones. Then, with reference to "the incarnation of our Lord Jesus Christ," we find a denial of the Apollinarian heresy in "Perfect God, and perfect man." Nestorianism however is rejected in "Who, although he be God and man: yet he is not two, but one Christ." And finally, the monophysites are challenged by "One altogether: not by confusion of substance." No doubt we can get along without saying or singing this Creed often, or even at all. It will not hurt us to ponder it, and to try to understand its intent and its content.

Augustine had concluded his Trinitarian treatise, as now this chapter well may conclude, with an emphatic reminder that it is not logical subtlety, but Christian experience and devotion, which make the doctrine of the Trinity worth considering, and for believers inevitable for believing. "Lift thine eyes to the light itself," he urged, "and fix them upon it, if thou canst. Then only shalt thou see the difference of the begetting of God's Word from the procession of God's Gift." Therefore he brought

> this Book at last to an end, not with argument but with prayer: When therefore we shall have attained to thee, all those many things which we speak, and attain not, shall cease: one shalt thou abide, all things in all; one shall we name thee without end, praising thee with one single voice, we ourselves also made one in thee.[23]

Not yet then, and not yet today, do we see all Christians made one. Yet the essential formulation of agreed Christian teaching about the nature of God, as held and taught alike in the East and the West, and later in the Protestant North, was established and ratified at Chalcedon. We turn now to notice both continuity and challenge as the course of history has moved to our own time.

IX. *IN ESSENTIA UNITAS*

The Feast of the Trinity, set on the Sunday after Whit-sunday, was originated by Stephen, Bishop of Liège from 903 to 920. It quickly gained popularity in the Low Countries, but spread only slowly thence into the rest of Europe. Its observance in England was authorized by St. Thomas à Becket in the latter part of the twelfth century. Trinity Sunday was not officially sanctioned for the whole Western Church until 1334, in the reign of Pope John XXII.

The Roman Catholic "Preface of the Most Holy Trinity," of which both the Lutheran and the Anglican Proper Prefaces for Trinity Sunday are condensations, is much older than the feast itself. Its authorship is ascribed to Pope Pelagius II, who reigned from 579 to 590, immediately before St. Gregory the Great. In the Gregorian Sacramentary this Preface was assigned to the first Sunday after Pentecost, which of course is the day that ultimately the West settled on for the Trinity observance.

Said regularly in the Roman Mass on "all Sundays to which no special (Preface) is assigned," it reads:

> Who, together with Thine only-begotten Son and the Holy Ghost, art one God, one Lord, not in the singleness of one Person, but in the Trinity of one substance. For that which, according to Thy revelation, we believe of Thy glory, the same we believe of thy Son, the same of the Holy Ghost, without difference or distinction; so that in the confession of one true and eternal Godhead we adore distinctness in persons, oneness in essence, and equality in majesty.[1]

In 1928 the Protestant Episcopal Church in the United

States, apparently growing nervous already about its phrasing, "in Trinity of Persons and in Unity of Substance," provided for the day an alternate Preface which does mention the three Persons, even if a bit casually, but manages to avoid any naming of the Trinity as such. In its support one may note that it is (a) scriptural, and (b) brief:

> For the precious death and merits of thy Son Jesus Christ our Lord, and for the sending to us of the Holy Ghost, the Comforter; who are one with thee in thy Eternal Godhead.[2]

It may or may not be regarded as a further defense that this twentieth-century formula accords fully with the fifth-century "blasphemy of Sirmium" in its complete elimination of the term "substance." [3]

The original Latin of the historic Preface uses both *substantia* and *essentia,* as the English version indicates: "the Trinity of one *substantia,*" and "oneness in *essentia.*" Manifestly there is intended here no real "difference or distinction" between the two terms. The Latin phrase *in essentia unitas,* "oneness in essence," is of course to be distinguished from its familiar homophone, *in essentiis unitas,* "unity in essentials." The latter refers to relationships human rather than divine. Yet a possible confusion of the two is not seriously to be regretted. If the Godhead is one in essence, then (even as Augustine pointed out almost two centuries before Pelagius wrote)[4] oneness among the people of God would seem to be a reasonable corollary.

There was to all intents and purposes unity of thought about the Trinity throughout the later Middle Ages. In general the pattern of thinking in the West continued to be Augustinian. Early in the ninth century we find Claudius, the vigorous and somewhat contentious Bishop of Turin, citing Augustine's *On the Trinity*.[5] Three hundred years later Rupert of Deutz, near Cologne, says of the Word that "He was with God as wisdom is with a wise man, as might with a mighty man," and then goes on to speak of "that love which is the Holy Spirit." [6]

St. Anselm of Canterbury, in the classic *Cur Deus Homo* (properly not "Why God Became Man," but "Why a Godman?"), says that "the Son of God . . . offered his humanity to his divinity, which is itself one of the three persons." [7] Richard of St. Victor is fully Augustinian in interpretation, as well as thoroughly a scholastic in style, when he argues that

> . . . no person could be wholly deserving of the love of a divine person if he were not God. Therefore, in order for the fullness of charity to have its place in that true divinity, it is necessary for any divine person not to lack divine fellowship. Observe, then, how easily reason proves that plurality of persons cannot be lacking in the true divinity. . . the fullness of goodness could not have existed without the fullness of charity, nor the fullness of charity without the plurality of divine persons.[8]

Nor should we forget that we owe to this period also Peter Abelard's *O Quanta Qualia,* with the Trinitarian doxology which this intellectual rebel used regularly to close his hymns in this meter:

> Low before Him with our praises we fall,
> Of whom, and in whom, and through whom are all;
> Of whom, the Father; and through whom, the Son;
> In whom, the Spirit, with them ever One.[9]

Decisively as the Aristotelian methodology of St.

Thomas Aquinas differed from the basic Platonism of St. Augustine, the author of the *Summa Theologica* proposed no innovations in the interpretation of the Trinity. Nor did such "reformers before the Reformation" as John Wycliffe, John Hus, and Erasmus of Rotterdam. Hus made Trinitarianism his point of reference in his attack on three practical "heresies" which he saw in the Church. "With these three heresies," he protested,

> the entire Holy Trinity is contemned: God the Father is contemned by apostasy, for he rules mightily by a pure and immaculate law . . . God the Son, who is the Wisdom of God, is contemned by the second heresy—blasphemy; and God the Holy Spirit, who in his supreme goodness wisely and humbly governs God's house, is contemned by the accursed simony which is contrary to his order.[10]

Even the successful revolutions of the Protestants in the sixteenth century involved no significant controversy in this area. The Augsburg Confession of 1530 presented no conflict with what had become standard Trinitarian doctrine, though it was outspoken in its challenges to the Roman Church at many other points. "Our churches with one accord teach," it said at the very beginning of its Article I, "Of God, the Most Holy Trinity,"

> agreeably to the Council of Nice, that there is only one Divine Being, which is called, and verily is, GOD, but that there are three persons in this Divine Being, equally powerful, equally eternal, God the Father, God the Son, and God the Holy Ghost, who are one Divine Being, eternal, incorporeal, indivisible, infinite in power, wisdom, and goodness, one Creator and Preserver of all visible and invisible things. And the term *person* is not to be understood to signify a part or quality of something

else, but that which exists of itself, as also the Fathers have made use of this term on this subject.[11]

In a sermon for Trinity Sunday Martin Luther himself told his congregation that

> the Creed confesses three persons as comprehended in one divine essence, each one, however, retaining his distinct personality; and in order that the simple Christian may recognize that there is but one divine essence and one God, who is tri-personal, a special work, peculiar to himself, is ascribed to each person. And such acts, peculiar to each person, are mentioned for the reason that thus a confusion of persons is avoided. To the Father we ascribe the work of creation; to the Son the work of Redemption; to the Holy Spirit the power to forgive sins, to gladden, to strengthen, to transport from death to life eternal.
>
> The thought is not that the Father alone is the Creator, the Son alone Redeemer and the Holy Spirit alone Sanctifier. . . . All these are operations of the one Divine Majesty as such. . . . Such distinction is made for the purpose of affording the unqualified assurance that there is but one God and yet three persons in the one divine essence.[12]

Here indeed there is nothing revolutionary. Rather there are clear echoes both of Origen in the third century and of Anselm in the eleventh.[13]

Almost at the outset of his *Institutes,* John Calvin, discussing the Latin *personae* and the Greek *hypostases,* argues that "to wrangle over this clear matter is undue squeamishness and even obstinacy . . . Although they . . . differ among themselves over the word, yet they quite agree in the essential matter." He defends the word "Trinity" also, as necessary to "render the truth plain and clear," and as "especially useful when the truth is to be asserted against false accusers." He is completely in accord with the decrees of Nicea, Constantinople, and Chalcedon, supporting the *homoousios* and assailing both Arius and Sabellius as if he were Athanasius himself.[14]

The Westminster Confession of Faith, adopted by the English Calvinists in 1646, had as its second chapter a statement "Of God and of the Holy Trinity." "In the unity of the Godhead," it said,

> there be three persons, of one substance, power, and eternity; God the Father, God the Son, and God the Holy Ghost. The Father is of none, neither begotten nor proceeding; the Son is eternally begotten of the Father; the Holy Ghost eternally proceeding from the Father and the Son.[15]

Here are echoes not only of Nicea and of Chalcedon, but also of *Quicunque vult.*

Even the much more radical Congregationalists were quite content with this. In their "Declaration of Faith and Order" adopted in 1658 they but added to the Westminster statement, "Which Doctrine of the Trinity is the foundation of all our Communion with God, and comfortable Dependence upon him." [16]

With Lutherans, Calvinists, and Independents thus accepting and defending the standard Trinitarian doctrine, it is not surprising to find that the less theologically concerned Church of England presented no divergence either. The Articles of Religion adopted by the Parliament in 1571, and made binding on all the clergy under King James I in 1604, said that "in unity of this Godhead there be three Persons, of one substance, power, and eternity;

the Father, the Son, and the Holy Ghost." It spoke of "two whole and perfect Natures, that is to say, the Godhead and Manhood . . . joined together in one Person, never to be divided, whereof is one Christ, very God, and very Man." And it declared for the *filioque,* "the Holy Ghost, proceeding from the Father and the Son." [17] These expressions remain unchanged in the Articles of the Protestant Episcopal Church today, and also in the abbreviated Twenty-four Articles which John Wesley transmitted to the American Methodists in 1784.

It was during the first Reformation century, however, that new and vigorous denials of Trinitarian faith began to appear. Among the most notable was that of Michael Servetus, who was both a physician and a theologian. In 1531 he wrote *De Trinitatis Erroribus,* assailing not only the doctrine of the Trinity itself but also that of the Two Natures in the Christ. The unity between the Romans and the Reformers on the issue of the Trinity is dramatically and tragically reflected in Servetus' fate. Condemned by the Catholic authorities in Lyons, he escaped to Reformed Geneva. There, however, he was seized by the rulers of that city, and with Calvin's assent was burned as a heretic on October 27, 1553.

A longer career, and one of more lasting impact, was that of Faustus Socinus. A group of humanists in Italy, finding themselves in dissent from much of Catholic doctrine, had fled to Switzerland about the middle of the sixteenth century. There they came under the influence of Servetus, but upon his death sought shelter in Poland. In 1556 they organized themselves as the Minor Reformed

Church of Poland. In 1579 they were joined by Faustus Socinus, whose uncle Laelius Socinus had been associated with them in Italy and Switzerland, and had left a collection of his theological writings to his nephew. Faustus, depending on the sole authority of Scripture, interpreted it so as to deny both the Trinity and the Atonement.

The *Racovian Catechism,* composed in 1605 by Socinus' disciples, became a classic statement of anti-Trinitarian Christianity. It noted that "Christians commonly maintain, that, with the Father,—the SON and the HOLY SPIRIT are persons in one and the same Deity." Then it responded flatly that "in this they lamentably err." Admitting that the Scriptures teach "the existence of the Father, Son, and Holy Spirit," it contended that "these testimonies do not prove the matter in dispute; namely, that the Father, Son, and Holy Spirit, are three persons in the one essence of God." Discussing I Corinthians 12:4-6, it argued that

> although divine operations are here attributed to God, to the Lord, (who is Christ), and also to the Holy Spirit, it cannot be hence proved that these three are the one God. Indeed the direct contrary is to be inferred from the passage; since the Lord, (that is Christ), and the Holy Spirit, are most clearly distinguished by the apostle from the one God.[18]

The Socinians were driven out of Poland in 1658, after twenty preceding years of persecution by the Catholics. They found refuge variously in Transylvania, East Prussia, and the Netherlands. A Transylvanian movement, the first specifically called Unitarian, had broken away from the

Reformed Church in 1568. To this community the fleeing Socinians joined themselves, and soon lost their own identity as a group. The Unitarian Church in Transylvania, with the Socinian newcomers absorbed, persisted quietly through the years. Early in the nineteenth century it established fraternal relations with the Unitarian groups in Britain and America.

We know that the Racovian Catechism had found its way to England by 1614. In that year James I ordered the burning of a Latin version, although this had been dedicated to him by its translator. A small group known as "the Oxford latitudinarians," Lucius Cary, John Hales, and William Chillingworth, became familiar with some of the writings of Socinus, and in the first half of the seventeenth century spoke out for full freedom of theological discussion. Chillingworth is the author of the famous definition, "The Bible, and the Bible only, is the religion of Protestants." These latitudinarians were argued with, and occasionally reviled, but they were not actively persecuted.

The situation was quite different for "the father of the English Unitarians." This was John Biddle, an Oxford man who arrived at non-Trinitarian views through his own study of the Scriptures. Upon the publication (1647) of his *Twelve Arguments Drawn from Scripture,* he was imprisoned, and the book was ceremonially burned by the public hangman. In 1654 he was exiled by Cromwell. On Cromwell's death in 1658 Biddle returned, but in 1662 he was arrested by the Restoration authorities and soon afterward died in prison. (One notes, however reluctantly, the full agreement in belligerent Trinitarianism be-

111

tween the English Parliamentarians and the Royalists, who agreed on practically nothing else.)

It is now known that John Milton, who had moved from Anglicanism through Presbyterianism to Independency, arrived at what was essentially an Arian position before the end of his career. His *De Doctrina Christiana,* probably written about 1660, was not published until 1825: the reason no doubt being its forthright expression of what were regarded as quite intolerable heresies. The full title of the treatise, in English, is *John Milton, an Englishman, His Christian Doctrine, Compiled from the Holy Scriptures Alone.* This suggests that Milton was familiar with, and affected by, the Socinian point of view: an impression which is supported by the fact that there are many affinities between Milton's arguments and the Racovian Catechism.[19]

"However the generation of the Son may have taken place," said Milton,

> it arose from no natural necessity, as is generally contended. . . . For questionless, it was in God's power consistently with the perfection of his own essence not to have begotten the Son, inasmuch as generation does not pertain to the nature of the Deity, who stands in no need of propagation. . . .
>
> God imparted to the Son as much as he pleased of the divine nature, nay of the divine substance itself, care being taken not to confound the substance with the whole essence. . . .
>
> Christ has received his fulness from God, in the sense in which we shall receive our fulness from Christ. . . . He declares himself to be one with the Father in the same manner as we are one with him: that is, not in essence,

but in love, in communion, in agreement, in charity, in spirit, in glory. . . .
The Son likewise teaches that the attributes of divinity belong to the Father alone, to the exclusion even of himself.[20]

Milton went into hiding at the Restoration of 1660, but was included in the general amnesty which followed. It was in 1665 that he completed "Paradise Lost," whose failure to support the orthodox doctrine of the Trinity scarcely was noticed until the *De Doctrina* became known in the nineteenth century.

With the "Glorious Revolution" of 1688 there was a general suspension of persecution on theological grounds. In the last years of the century the English "Socinians" and the defenders of orthodoxy debated the Trinitarian issue with a good deal of heat, here and there a bit of light, and no bloodshed. Discussion continued into the eighteenth century, whose latitudinarianism permitted quite free expression of minority opinions. In 1774, in London, there was held the first service of what may properly be called a Unitarian congregation.

Disorders did follow, with the covert approval of a few Church authorities, when some of England's religious liberals were found (or alleged) to be sympathetic with the Revolution in France. In Birmingham both the Unitarian meetinghouse and the residence of its minister, Dr. Joseph Priestley, were wrecked and burned by mobs in 1791. The year 1819 saw the formation of the Unitarian Association for Protecting the Civil Rights of Unitarians. In 1825 this was merged with the Unitarian Fund to become the British and Foreign Unitarian Association. Thus Unitarianism in Britain became a full-fledged dissenting denomination.

Benjamin Franklin had attended that first London Unitarian service in 1774. Unitarianism in the United States, however, seems to have developed in general quite independently of direct influences from Britain. King's Chapel in Boston, the oldest Anglican Church in New England, revised the *Book of Common Prayer* for its own use in 1785, eliminating all references to the Trinity. (For the *Gloria Patri,* for example, it substituted the ascription from I Timothy, "Now unto the king immortal, eternal, invisible . . ." [21]) The newly formed Protestant Episcopal Church refused to recognize this congregation, and so drove it into association with the non-Trinitarian thinkers who were arising in the Congregational Churches.

In 1797 a group of fourteen English Unitarians, who had settled in Pennsylvania, organized The First Society of Unitarian Christians in Philadelphia. Harvard University became known as a disseminator of "liberal" or "Arian" views, and rapidly peopled the Massachusetts pulpits with ministers who cared little for the orthodox formulae. The great liberal leader in Boston was William Ellery Channing of the Federal Street Church. A sermon which he preached in Baltimore in 1819 made so eloquent a defence of the Unitarian position that it crystalized both opposition and support. The American Unitarian Association was organized in 1825, and retained that identity until its merger with the Universalists in 1961 in the Unitarian Universalist Association.

It seems clear that Trinitarianism as such was scarcely

the issue either in England or in America. In England "Socinianism" commonly was identified much less in specific theological terms than as an attitude of general toleration. As to the theology, one gathers that what most of the "Unitarian" leaders were opposing was less a genuine Trinitarianism than an effective and naïve tritheism.

The principal point of controversy, however, was that over the nature of Jesus Christ. Not only was his equality with God disputed, but now also his standing in any special relationship to the Father. He was recognized as a supreme teacher and a heroic servant of mankind, but as only one (though perhaps the finest) among many human beings who had contributed to man's clearer thinking and nobler living.

We scarcely may claim that either the intellectual or the moral responses of the orthodox denominations were impressive. In general the Trinitarians satisfied themselves (but certainly not their opponents) by citing the authority of Scripture and Creeds, and now and then by attempting to use the authority of regulations and penalties. As to the nature of Christ, the prevailing response to Socinianism was a revived and very crude Apollinarianism. Attempts to do any explaining in terms of new categories of thought and new points of reference were few and far between.

One of these few developments came from a secular rather than an ecclesiastical source. It was the applying by Friedrich Hegel of his basic dialectic to a triune structuring of his Absolute. In this the Father is to be identified as thesis, the Son as antithesis, and the Spirit as synthesis. Hegel saw this against the background of an evolutionary process leading from the primitive nature religions to the Absolute Religion of Christianity, a process in which the divine Reality takes part and in which it is itself eternally realized. "The reconciliation believed in as being in Christ," Hegel urged,

> has no meaning if God is not known as Trinity, if it is not recognized that He *is* but is at the same time the Other, the self-differentiation, the Other in the sense that this Other is God Himself and has potentially the divine nature in it, and that the abolishing of this difference, of this otherness, this return, this love, is Spirit.[22]

Early in the present century there arose a school of what may be called a "social interpretation" of the Trinity. "We have a social humanity," wrote Dr. George A. Gordon of Old South Church in Boston. "Have we a social Deity as the ground of it?" "The Christian doctrine of the Trinity," he suggested,

> is the full statement of the truth at which Greek mythology aimed; the discovery of the social nature of God through the social nature of man at his highest. Put into the Godhead some reality answering to the words the Father, and the Son, and the Holy Spirit, and one is able to think of the divine knowledge and love as real, one is able to conceive of God's existence as ineffably blessed, and as containing in itself the ground of human society.[23]

Similarly the English J. R. Illingworth argued that "the doctrine of the Trinity first comes to us by way of personal experience." "How is it," he asked,

> that we really come into immediate contact with the Christian creed in our own experience at the present day? Not primarily as a doctrine at all, but as a living and breathing and organised society of men and women all

around us, whose creed is only the intellectual explanation of their actual life. And that actual life consists in the conviction of those who are sincerely living it, in progressive communion with the Father, through fellowship in the mystical body of His Son, effected by the operation of the Holy Spirit within them.

"The doctrines in question," he says at the conclusion of his book on the Trinity, "have been for nigh twenty centuries, and still are at the present day, through the living agency of the Christian society, the foremost force in the spiritual world." [24]

A more systematic exposition of this general concept is that of Leonard Hodgson, presented in his Croall lectures at Edinburgh in 1943. Hodgson points out that mathematical unity and organic unity are not identical, and that a meaningful organic unity almost of necessity embraces diversity within it. Using the analogy of human selfhood, he sounds a good deal like St. Augustine in his discussion of thinking, feeling, and willing as distinct yet unified aspects of personality. He does not attempt to assign these functions severally and separately to the three Persons of the Trinity, but he does imply that some such analysis may be pertinent enough to reflect the truth.

At the same time, Hodgson definitely treats "the constituent elements in the Godhead" as being "intelligent, purposive centres of consciousnesss." This he supports by "the projection into eternity" of the relationships among Father, Son, and Spirit as seen in the incarnation and in the history of the Church: "the assertion that eternally the Divine Life is a life of mutual self-giving to one another of Father and Son through the Spirit who is the *vinculum* or bond of love between them." [25] Whether or not this avoids an eternal tritheism would seem to depend on whether or not there was a temporary tritheism in the first century.

Manifestly these attempts to identify the Trinity in social terms reflect not only the characteristic emphases of the ancient Eastern Fathers, but also the *Zeitgeist* of the "social gospel" of the early years of this century. Just as manifestly, every attempt to interpret has been, and any attempt will be, similarly conditioned by the spirit and the culture of its own time. So far we have limited ourselves, as far as might be, to remembrance of times past. It remains now to ask what we may reasonably think, and believe, and say, and live by, in our own day. Does the doctrine of the Holy Trinity reflect and express any reality for us? If so, wherein does that reality consist? Is there a unity in essence such as can bring us into oneness ourselves?

The Realities

THIS LAST section is headed "Continuance" rather than "Conclusion," because in the case of the Holy Trinity there can be no ending of experience, and there should be no ending of enquiry or of efforts at interpretation. It is not with static formulae, but with vital and vitalizing reality, that we have been and are concerned. It is in the eternal continuance of that reality that we must live.

Experience is by its very nature infallible. Interpretation by its very nature is fallible indeed. That distinction I first heard pointed out by the late Dr. Wilfred R. H. Hodgkin, at evensong in St. Mark's Church in Berkeley, California, in the summer of 1924. I have never forgotten his sermon, and I have seen ever increasing reasons for accepting and reasserting its truth.

Nowhere is the principle more apposite than in the area of theology. The facts of religious experience are undeniable. What has happened to us, to all of us or to any one of us, has happened; and that is that. What caused it, what it means, what it teaches us, what we ought to do about it, are different questions altogether. Our attempts to answer them may be wholly right, or wholly wrong, or (and more probably) partly wrong and partly right.

Recognizing our fallibility in interpretation does not relieve us of the right, or of the duty, to keep on trying to interpret. The more difficult it is to be sure of rightness, the more strenuously must we seek to avoid or conquer error. It is the very difficulty of the Trinitarian problem which requires us to do all that we can toward its understanding and its (even though very partial) solving.

This time it will be convenient to return to the familiar order of mention, asking ourselves about the First, Second, and Third Persons of the Trinity in the sequence in which usually they have been listed. Is the Father real? And the Son? And the Spirit? If we answer "Yes," then we may be ready to essay a judgment as to their interrelationships.

The ultimate question about the Father, and the one which the "Death of God" theologians manage skilfully to ignore, is whether there is in this universe any ultimate at all. Let us grant that the issue lends itself neither to laboratory demonstration nor to logical proof on either side. Then let us ask whether it makes more sense to assume an eternity which includes time but transcends it, or to regard the phenomena of this time world as themselves a series of successive surrogates for eternity.

It is this very time-world that is too much with us, and that tricks us so often into laying waste our powers. Rejecting the "primordial" Being as irrelevant, the "Christian atheists" condemn themselves to imprisonment in a recurring series of unrelated temporaries. This may be their privilege; but it does not authorize them to insist that all the world shall share this incarceration.

The world of calculable time is also that of measurable

space. In neither of these is the ground of being fully and truly to be recognized. Not in the starry heavens above (nor even "around"), but in the moral law within, do the timeless values present themselves to us. Without eternal truth and right there can be no right or truth worth bothering about in time and space.

It is not irrational to suppose a God who created things material and temporary. It scarcely is rational to deny a Creator of things spiritual and enduring. God may be conceived as the maker of heaven and earth. He is inescapable as the Father of our spirits.

Is this God personal? Obviously he is incorporeal, but that is beside the point. Personality is identity, awareness, remembering, thinking, feeling, willing, acting. Personality, thus recognized, is the supreme treasure we have known on earth. In these terms surely we must believe that the Father of all is at least personal. If he were not, he would be less significant than we are. How much more than personal God is, we are not qualified to say.

The forms of description handed down to us from the past are necessarily inadequate, as any forms must be that we ourselves devise. The old forms still may be used: used not to express, and certainly not to enclose, but in some measure to reflect, what we have glimpsed of the invisible and what we have apprehended of the inexpressible. Therefore we may speak, in humility and yet in confidence, of the Lord of Israel and of the Father of all mankind. They who speak thus, and believing, can not but offer themselves to obey him and to serve him.

We who are Christian are persuaded also that the timeless ultimate has been revealed in time, to as many as are willing to receive him. That revelation we see both in Jesus in the first century and in the Holy Spirit in every century. What now shall we think of Christ?

Richard Watson Gilder posed, in "The Song of a Heathen," what has seemed to many to be an unavoidable antithesis:

> If Jesus Christ is a man—
>   And only a man,—I say
> That of all mankind I cleave to him,
>   And to him will I cleave alway.
>
> If Jesus Christ is a god—
>   And the only God,—I swear
> I will follow him through heaven and hell,
>   The earth, the sea, and the air!

What is wrong here, and in each of the two quatrains, is the implication of the word "only." To say that Jesus Christ was a man does not have to mean that he was "only a man." To call him a god may identify him with "the only God," but it does not require us to hold that he was "only a God."

To begin with that last, we must repudiate, flatly and eagerly, the revived Appollinarianism which appears both in current fundamentalist teaching and in the unexamined supposing (I do not say "thinking") of many lay Christians. The notion that Jesus was totally God, making temporary use of a human body, robs his presence among men of all moral value and of every saving grace. If he knew all things, the agony of the cross was fraudulent. If he could not have been truly and fiercely tempted in the wilderness, he could and can offer no succour to us who are tempted.

The human nature and human experience of the Christ are critical to his relevance to humanity, even as Paul and the writer of Hebrews saw and argued nineteen centuries ago. Yet if one jumps from the Apollinarian extreme to the Unitarian (or liberal modernist) one, he is simply moving from one inadequacy to another. Our Lord was a man, but he was not "only a man."

He was a man such as the world never had known, and could not have invented. He fulfilled not the national hopes of Israel, but the personal needs of all men and women everywhere. Many a Hellenistic Saviour-God had proffered salvation from punishment. This Jewish teacher far surpassed that, for he provided redemption from sin.

A devout Jew, seeing all this, had to respond by calling him not "just a man," but God's own Messiah. A simple pagan could conclude only that "this man was the Son of God." A philosopher was driven to realize that the eternal, life-giving *logos* had been made flesh and dwelt among us.[1]

Again the traditional categories are far from adequate, but again they are far from useless. This Galilean man compels us to see him also as expressing that moral and spiritual ultimate whom we have called "God." There is therefore not only reason, but also necessity, in what the Church has said about the two-nature doctrine. Chalcedon has phrased the inescapable conclusion: "perfect in Godhead . . . perfect in manhood, truly God and truly man

. . . consubstantial with the Father in Godhead, and the same consubstantial with us in manhood." [2]

The revelation of God in his continuing creation, and his revelation in his incarnate Son, are accompanied by the revelation which comes unendingly in the presence of his Spirit. That Spirit, as we have seen, was recognized by Judaism long before the first Christian century. In that century too, and in all those that have followed, something has occurred and recurred that cannot otherwise be explained than by the dwelling of the infinite in the minds and hearts and lives of finite folk.

Love, courage, and self-sacrifice are natural to no animal, and certainly not to the human one. Nature, despite all our romanticizing about it, is red in tooth and claw. Human nature is an evident and sufficient argument for the reality of original sin. The Christ opened the way for our being saved from that death which is our sinfulness. It is the divine Spirit, whose coming Jesus promised, who strengthens us to endure in the life of righteousness.

We believe then in God the Father Almighty. We believe in Jesus Christ, his only Son, our Lord. We believe in the Holy Spirit. Does this mean that we believe in the Holy Trinity? Are we clear yet as to whether we believe in three gods, or truly in one?

It must be admitted that it is possible to hold to a high Christology, and to be fully sensitive to the operation of the Holy Spirit, while refusing assent to the doctrine of the Trinity as such. Alexander Campbell of the Disciples of Christ provides a nineteenth-century example, and Cyril Richardson of Union Seminary a current one.[3] Yet it is hard to see how, if one recognizes the divine in the Son and in the Spirit, one can avoid some attempt to formulate their relationship to the Father: that is, something essentially equivalent to Trinitarian doctrine.

Tritheism can not be the answer. There are not three separate divine individuals who sit side by side on three thrones and discuss the state of the universe. That universe is one, and its ground of being must be one. Nor are the functions of Father, Son, and Holy Spirit so distinct one from another as to permit their neat distribution among three discrete entities. God is one essence, one *ousia,* whom we have found and identified in three *hypostases.*

The Sabellian solution, contrasting sharply with tritheism, is an attractive one to the modern mind. In two recent books Henry P. Van Dusen cites as from Harry Emerson Fosdick, and then Walter Russell Bowie cites from Van Dusen, an analogy seen in Theodore Roosevelt.[4] That ebullient individual was the President of the United States. He was an adventurer, and a writer about his adventures. He was the happy father of a picturesquely happy family. These were at least three manifestations of Roosevelt's personality. Yet he was one person, and only one.

If we try to apply this type of analysis to the Almighty, we may find it good so far as it goes. It does account for diversity of expression without denying unity of essence. Thus it protects monotheistic thinking, and precludes any disposition toward a pluralistic and disintegrating superstition.

So far as it goes: but surely it does not go far enough. This neo-Sabellianism fails adequately to describe, let alone to account for, the richness of experience we have found in successive and continuing involvements with Father, Son, and Holy Ghost. With reference to the passion of our Lord, it leaves the way open either for a new Patripassianism or for a sentimental Unitarianism. It was not God the Father who died on the cross, but neither was it merely a gallant man.

As in the problem of God's personality, we have to respond here again in terms of "at least." It is true that the three *personae* are three manifestations of the one divine essence. That certainly is not all they are, either in logic or in Christian life. The Word can not be limited to thirty years in the first century, though it was then that he was made flesh. The Spirit is not only everlasting, but also eternal: coming to us at all times, but existent beyond all times.

Here we need also to consider the *filioque.* The Spirit proceeds from the Father: of that Judaism was in no more doubt than Eastern Orthodoxy has been. But we who have known the Spirit dwelling among us and in us need not depend upon either a proof-text or a Creed to know that the Spirit has proceeded to us not only from the eternal Father, but from the incarnate Son as well. "Hereby we know that he abideth in us, by the Spirit which he hath given us." [5] We accept that, not because the Johannine author said it but because we have experienced it.

Thus the Trinitarian pattern attains its own full circle. The eternal Spirit proceeds eternally from the eternal Father and the eternal Son. Equally the Spirit is the Father here present with us, and the Son who equated the Spirit's coming with his own return. It is by and in the Spirit that we in time and space have been permitted to know both the Everlasting Father and the Prince of Peace. This is the truth expressed in the *per ipsum* of the Roman and Anglican Prayers of Consecration, which now Rome calls on the priest to say loudly and triumphantly for all to hear: "by whom, and with whom, in the unity of the Holy Ghost, all honour and glory be unto thee, O Father Almighty, world without end." [6] It is in the unity of the Holy Ghost that the Trinity is one.

Is there any necessary "threeness"? There is no absolute necessity for it which we may insist on. We do not know, and cannot know, all the internal economy of the eternal. The Church conceivably might have analyzed otherwise, arriving at numbers of two, or four, or almost any other. We do know that it came to recognize and to rejoice in three expressions of the divine, and to believe at once in their distinctness and in their oneness. So far, no one has made an accounting which accords better with the known experience.

The essence is one, and the Holy Trinity is one in essence. The manifestations are three of whom we can speak out of our own experience of them, whether or not there are or could be absolutely more than three. The doctrine of the Trinity is our attempt to describe and to understand what ultimately we do not understand and cannot describe. We have not already attained, and our formulations are far from being made perfect.

The experience of the Trinity yet is within our grasp. We know that, for we have known it in our lives. As we reach forward to the things which are before, as we press toward the mark for the prizes of fuller revelation and fuller realization, we may give thanks for the doctrine which has helped so much to make our present realizings clear to our own minds. Then, and much more importantly, we shall give thanks to the Holy Trinity, Father, Son, and Holy Ghost, for the revelations which have lifted our spirits and the grace which has transformed our lives.

These are realities which we can not deny. This, therefore, is a doctrine which helpfully we may use.

Notes

LIST OF ABBREVIATIONS

ANF . . . *The Ante-Nicene Fathers* (Buffalo, 1885 and after).

DCC . . . Henry Bettenson, editor, *Documents of the Christian Church* (London, second edition 1963).

LCC . . . *The Library of Christian Classics* (Philadelphia, 1953 and after).

LCL . . . *Loeb Classical Library* (London, 1912 and after).

NPNF . . . *A Select Library of Nicene and Post-Nicene Fathers of the Christian Church* (New York, second series 1890 and after).

PG   . . . J. P. Migne, editor, *Patrologiae Cursus Completus,* Greek series (Paris, 1857 and after).

PL   . . . The same, Latin series (Paris, 1844 and after).

Introduction: THE CHALLENGES

[1] John A. T. Robinson, *Honest to God* (Philadelphia, 1963).

[2] James A. Pike, *A Time for Christian Candor* (New York, 1964).

[3] Cyril C. Richardson, *The Doctrine of the Trinity* (New York, 1958).

[4] See Gabriel Vahanian, *The Death of God: the Culture of Our Post-Christian Era* (New York, 1961); Paul Van Buren, *The Secular Meaning of the Gospel* (New York, 1963); Thomas J. J. Altizer and William Hamilton, *Radical Theology and the Death of God* (Indianapolis, 1966); William Hamilton, *The New Essence of Christianity* (New York, 1966); Thomas J. J. Altizer, *The Gospel of Christian Atheism* (Philadelphia, 1966).

THE BACKGROUNDS

1. Plurality to Unity

[1] Deuteronomy 6:4.

[2] Thus both the "Conservative" *Standard Prayer Book* (New York, 1915) and the "Reform" *Union Prayerbook for Jewish Worship* (Cincinnati, revised edition 1940), in harmony with the rendering in *The Holy Scriptures According to the Masoretic Text: a New Translation* (Philadelphia, 1917).

[3] *The Torah: the Five Books of Moses, a New Translation of the Holy Scriptures According to the Masoretic Text, First Section* (Philadelphia, 1962).

[4] Exodus 20:7; Deuteronomy 5:11. In all probability this was neither a prohibition of oral profanity, as Christendom usually has understood it, nor a taboo on the saying of the word itself, as in the traditional Jewish use; but simply a requirement that prayer always should be accompanied by sacrifice: "Thou shalt not call on the Lord when thou art empty-handed."

[5] Exodus 3:13-15.

[6] Exodus 6:3. This account belongs probably to the fifth century B.C. Here the new Jewish *Torah* version does use the name itself, but in Hebrew rather than Roman characters.

[7] Genesis 4:26.

[8] See Exodus 18:14-18, 20:18-21. Cf. I Samuel 7:10; 12:18; Isaiah 29:6.

[9] Judges 6:10; I Samuel 5.

[10] Judges 2:11-12; 11:24; I Kings 11:5, 7.

[11] I Kings 11:6.

[12] Jeremiah 50:2. Cf. II Kings 25:7; Isaiah 39:1; Jeremiah 52:31; where the name appears in the combinations Merodach-baladan and Evil-merodach.

[13] Genesis 1:1—2:4. Babylonian elements include the familiar "three-tier" universe, and also the sexagesimal system of numeration.

[14] Genesis 2:4b-25.

[15] Amos 1:3-8, 13-15; 2:1-3. The sections relating to Tyre, Edom, and Judah, 1:9-12 and 2:4-5, are of doubtful authenticity. Probably they were interpolated by much later hands.

[16] Amos 2:6. The specifications of Israel's wrongdoing occupy most of the remainder of the book.

[17] Hosea 11:8-9; 14:4.

[18] Isaiah 45:1, 5-7.

[19] See Zechariah 3:1f; I Chronicles 21:1; Job 1:6—2:7. References to "the Satan" (with the definite article in the Greek, except in the vocative) are comparatively numerous in the Gospels, the epistles of St. Paul, and the Revelation of St. John.

II. The Spirit of the Lord

[1] Genesis 3:8-12; 18:1-33.

[2] Genesis 22:11-19; Exodus 14:19; 23:20, 23; 32:34; 33:2; Judges 2:1-5; 6:11-24; 13:2-23.

[3] The "E" portions are Genesis 28:11-12, 17-18, 20-22; the "J" are Genesis 28:10, 13-16, 19.

[4] Ezekiel 37:1-10, 14.

[5] Genesis 1:2; Job 26:13; 4:9.

[6] Genesis 6:3; 41:38; Exodus 31:2-3; 35:30-31; Numbers 11:29.

[7] Judges 3:10; 6:34; 11:29; 13:25; 14:6, 19; 15:14.

[8] I Samuel 10:6, 10-11; 16:13-14; II Samuel 23:1-2.

[9] Isaiah 11:2; 42:1; Micah 3:8.

[10] Ezekiel 11:24; 37:1, 14; 39:29; 43:5; Joel 2:28; Acts 2:16-21 = Joel 2:28-32a.

[11] Zechariah 4:6.

[12] St. Luke 4:16-19 = Isaiah 61:1-2. One notes that either Jesus or the narrator saw fit to stop short of the next phrase: "and the day of vengeance of our God."

[13] Proverbs 8:1, 22-23; John 1:1-2.

[14] Wisdom 1:7; 9:17. The Greek in the latter is precisely *to hagion pneuma,* as in the usage of the New Testament. See, *e.g.,* Matthew 28:19; Luke 11:13; II Corinthians 13:14.

[15] Psalm 65:9.

[16] Philo, *On Dreams,* II.37; *On the Giants,* XI, XII. LCL (Philo) V, p. 553; II, pp. 469, 471.

[17] *On the Giants,* V. LCL (Philo) II, p. 457.

[18] Exodus 31:1-5; Numbers 11:16-17.

[19] Philo, *On the Giants,* V, VI. LCL (Philo) II, p. 459.

[20] Philo, *Questions and Answers on Genesis,* II.62. LCL (Philo) suppl. vol. I, pp. 150-51.

[21] Philo, *On Flight and Finding,* II. LCL (Philo) V, p. 17.

[22] See Chapter VIII herein.

[23] In Theodor H. Gaster, *The Dead Sea Scriptures* (Garden City, revised edition 1964) pp. 50, 100, 185, 187, 163, 360.

III. *Sons of God*

[1] Genesis 6:2, 4.

[2] Job 1:6.

[3] Hosea 11:1; Psalm 2:7.

[4] Heraclitus, Fragment 20. In Philip Wheelwright, *Heraclitus* (Princeton, 1959) pp. 29, 138.

[5] Fragment 1. Wheelwright, pp. 19, 134.

[6] Fragments 2, 64, 118. Wheelwright, pp. 19, 135; 68, 146; 102, 154.

[7] Epicharmus, Fragment 57. Clement of Alexandria, *Miscellanies,* V. xiv. ANF II, p. 471.

[8] Marcus Aurelius Antoninus, *Meditations,* I.8; VI.53; IV.15; VI.24. LCL (Marcus Aurelius) pp. 6, 184, 74, 142.

[9] Philo, *On the Posterity of Cain,* XXXVIII; *Concerning Noah's Work as a Planter,* II. LCL (Philo) II, p. 401; III, p. 217.

[10] John 1:14.

THE EXPERIENCE

[1] Arthur Cushman McGiffert, *The God of the Early Christians* (New York, 1924). See especially ch. II, pp. 41-88.

IV. *The Lord Incarnate*

[1] See The Commission of Appraisal (William Ernest Hocking, chairman), *Rethinking Missions: a Laymen's Inquiry After One Hundred Years* (New York, 1932).

[2] Acts 2:22, 36.

[3] See Irenaeus, *Against Heresies,* VI.1:3; Tertullian, *Prescriptions against Heretics,* 33. LCC I, p. 386; V, p. 55.

[4] Isaiah 45:1; Zechariah 4:14 (cf. all of chapters 3 and 4); Psalm 110. Note that both the Gospels and the Epistle to the

Hebrews apply this Psalm to our Lord (Mark 12:36 and parallels; Hebrews 1:13; chapters 5-7).

[5] Daniel 7:13-14.

[6] See I (Ethiopic) Enoch 52:4. R. H. Charles, *The Apocrypha and Pseudepigrapha of the Old Testament* (Oxford, 1913) II, p. 219.

[7] Cf. Acts 1:6.

[8] Zechariah 9:9f.

[9] Matthew 1:18-23, 2:15, 17f. Cf. Isaiah 7:10-16; Hosea 11:1-5; Jeremiah 31:15-17.

[10] See especially I Thessalonians 4:13-17.

[11] Revelation 11:15; 12:10; 20:4, 6.

[12] Cf. Mark 8:29 with Matthew 16:16 and Luke 9:20. In the last the "Western" Greek manuscripts read "Son of God" rather than "Christ of God."

[13] Matthew 1:20; Luke 1:35.

[14] Justin Martyr, *First Apology,* 21, 22. LCC I, pp. 255f.

[15] *Ibid.,* 33. LCC I, p. 263.

[16] Quoted by Epiphanius, *Against Heresies,* 72:2f. PG 42, pp. 385-388.

[17] See Rufinus, *Exposition of the Symbol.* PL 21, pp. 335-386.

[18] Hebrews 2:9-10; 3:6; 5:8; 1:1-2.

[19] Philippians 2:5-11.

[20] Cf. Fragments 1 and 64 of Heraclitus, and Philo's "everlasting Logos of the eternal God"; above, pp. 30.

[21] John 1:6-8, 12, 14; cf. I John 1:1.

[22] Letter to Diognetus 11:3, 5. LCC I, p. 222.

[23] Cf. above, p. 35. Justin, *First Apology,* 23, 32. LCC I, pp. 257, 262.

[24] Athenagoras, *Plea,* 10; Clement of Alexandria, *Miscellanies,* VII.7; Origen, *Dialogue with Heraclides,* 123. LCC I, p. 309; II, pp. 97, 438.

V. The Lord in Residence

[1] John 14:16-18.

[2] In the approximate order of their composition, I and II Thessalonians, Galatians, I and II Corinthians, Romans, Colossians, Philemon, Philippians. Excluded are I and II Timothy, Ephesians, and of course Hebrews.

[3] I Thessalonians 1:5; I Corinthians 2:13; 12:3.

[4] I Corinthians 12:8-11, 13; II Corinthians 13:14.

[5] Galatians 5:18-23.

[6] II Corinthians 3:2-3, 6, 17. The difference in the Greek of verse 17 would be only that between *kyriou* and *kyrion.*

[7] I Corinthians 14:2, 19. "Unknown" may of course be deleted throughout the chapter.

[8] Acts 2:4-13; 19:6.

[9] Acts 1:5; 4:8, 31; 7:55-56.

[10] Acts 8:18-24, 26, 29.

[11] Acts 10:44-48; 13:2-4, 19:6; 20:28; 21:11.

[12] Matthew 3:11—4:1; Mark 1:10-12; Luke 3:16-22; 4:1.

[13] Mark 3:29. Cf. Matthew 12:31-32; Luke 12:10.

[14] Revelation 1:10; 2:1-29; 3:1-22; 21:10; 22:17.

[15] John 7:39; 3:5; 4:24; 6:63.

[16] John 14:26; 16:8, 13f, 16.

[17] John 14:17.

[18] Athenagoras, *Plea,* 9. LCC I, p. 308. See also the long discussion by Justin in his *First Apology,* 30-60. LCC I, pp. 260-281. Approximately contemporary with Justin, and scarcely as rigid, is II Peter 1:21: "Holy men of God spake as they were moved by the Holy Ghost."

[19] Eusebius, *Church History,* V, xvi, 7f. NPNF I, p. 231. Hippolytus, *Refutation of All Heresies,* viii, 19. DCC p. 109.

[20] Tertullian, *On the Soul,* ix. DCC, pp. 109f. *On Modesty,* 21. LCC V, p. 75.

[21] Origen, *On Prayer,* II.6, XXXIII.3. LCC II, pp. 243, 329.

VI. The Lord Eternal

[1] Matthew 5:17.

[2] Isaiah 61:1 = Luke 4:18f. Cf. above, p. (15).

[3] Hosea 6:6 = Matthew 9:13; 12:7.

[4] Isaiah 29:13 = Mark 7:6-13.

[5] Mark 12:28-33. Jesus himself had of course been quoting from Deuteronomy 6:5 and Leviticus 19:18.

[6] Matthew 6:12, 14f; Mark 2:7; 11:25f; Luke 5:21; 11:4; 23:34.

[7] Matthew 5:22, 27-30; 18:9; 23:13-33; 25:41-46.

[8] Matthew 4:1-11; Luke 4:1-13; Deuteronomy 8:3; 6:13, 16.

[9] Mark 10:18; Luke 18:19; Matthew 19:17.

[10] Mark 2:1-12; Matthew 9:1-8; Luke 5:17-26; 7:36-50; 23:34; Matthew 27:46. Cf. Psalm 22:1.

[11] Matthew 11:27; Mark 13:32.

[12] II Samuel 20:23; I Kings 14:1; Numbers 1:9; I Samuel 9:1; Psalms 68:5; 103:13.

[13] Jeremiah 31:9; Isaiah 63:16; Malachi 2:10.

[14] John 5:18-23.

[15] John 14:6-9.

[16] II Corinthians 4:6; Colossians 1:15.

[17] I Thessalonians 1:9f; II Thessalonians 2:16; Galatians 4:6; I Corinthians 1:9; II Corinthians 1:3.

[18] Romans 1:1, 3f; Colossians 1:12f, 15; Philemon 3-5.

[19] Philippians 2:9-11.

[20] Cf. Thomas J. J. Altizer, *The Gospel of Christian Atheism* (Philadelphia, 1966) pp. 62-69.

[21] Hebrews 1:1; 13:20f; 11:1-40; Ecclesiasticus 44-49; Hebrews 12:1-2.

[22] Adolf Harnack, *History of Dogma* (transl. Neil Buchanan, Boston, 1899) I, p. 226.

[23] Irenaeus, *Against Heresies,* III.3:4. LCC I, p. 374.

[24] Justin, *First Apology,* 27. Cf. *ibid.,* 58. LCC I, pp. 258, 280.

[25] Irenaeus, *Against Heresies,* I.27:1f. LCC I, p. 367.

[26] *Ibid.,* I.27:2. LCC I, pp. 367-68.

[27] *Letter to Diognetus,* 7. LCC I, pp. 218-220.

[28] Athenagoras, *Plea,* 1, 2, 12. LCC I, pp. 308-09, 311. Cf. Exodus 20:2-3; Isaiah 44:6; 43:10-11; Proverbs 8:22.

[29] Irenaeus, *Against Heresies,* III.1:2; 5:3; 11:1, 6. LCC I, pp. 370, 377-78, 380. Cf. John 1:47-49; Matthew 12:18-20.

THE FORMULATION

VII. The Road to Nicea

[1] I John 5:7f.

[2] *The New Testament of our Lord and Savior Jesus Christ, Translated from the Latin Vulgate* (Paterson, New Jersey, 1941). *The New Testament of our Lord and Saviour Jesus*

Christ, translated (from the Greek) by the Very Reverend Francis Aloysius Spencer, O. P. (New York, 1937).

³ *The Sacred Writings of the Apostles and Evangelists of Jesus Christ, commonly styled the New Testament,* translated from the original Greek by Doctors George Campbell, James MacKnight, and Philip Doddridge (Grand Rapids, Michigan, reprinted 1951).

⁴ II Corinthians 13:14.

⁵ Romans 15:33; 16:27; Colossians 4:18; Philemon 25; Philippians 4:23.

⁶ Ephesians 6:23; Hebrews 13:20-21; I Timothy 6:21; Titus 3:15; II Timothy 4:22; I Peter 5:14; II Peter 3:18; Jude 20-21, 24-25.

⁷ Romans 8:9, 11.

⁸ Matthew 28:19.

⁹ Acts 2:30; 8:16; 19:5.

¹⁰ I Corinthians 6:11; 1:13; Galatians 3:27.

¹¹ *Didache,* 7:1-3. LCC I, p. 174.

¹² Justin, *First Apology,* 61. Irenaeus, *Against Heresies,* I.21:3. LCC I, pp. 282, 365.

¹³ Justin, *ibid.,* 13. LCC I, p. 249.

¹⁴ Athenagoras, *Plea,* 10. LCC I, pp. 308-09.

¹⁵ *Ibid.,* 10, 12, 24. LCC I, pp. 309, 311, 326.

¹⁶ Tertullian, *Against Praxeas,* II. ANF III, p. 598.

¹⁷ Tertullian, *On Baptism,* VI. ANF III, p. 672.

¹⁸ Cyprian, *Letter 73,* 5, 18. LCC V, pp. 160, 167.

¹⁹ Tertullian, *Against Praxeas,* I. ANF III, p. 597.

²⁰ Epiphanius, *Against Heresies,* LXII.1. DCC, p. 54.

²¹ Hebrews 1:3.

²² Jerome, *Letter 15.* LCC V, p. 309.

²³ Tertullian, *Against Praxeas,* X. ANF III, p. 604.

²⁴ Origen, *Dialogue with Heraclides,* 122-128. LCC II, pp. 438-39.

²⁵ Socrates, *Church History,* I.5. NPNF II, p. 3.

²⁶ Arius to Eusebius of Nicomedia. In Epiphanius, *Against Heresies,* LXIX. 7. LCC III, p. 330.

²⁷ "Confession of the Arians." In Epiphanius, *loc. cit.* LCC III, pp. 333-34.

[28] Letter to Eusebius of Caesarea, A.D. 325. In Athanasius, *On the Decrees of Nicaea.* LCC III, p. 337.

[29] *Ibid.* LCC III, p. 338.

[30] *Ibid.* LCC III, p. 339.

VIII. Disputings and Definings

[1] Athanasius, *On the Synods,* 23. DCC, pp. 58f.

[2] Socrates, *Church History,* II.30. NPNF, II, p. 56.

[3] Athanasius, *On the Synods,* 8. DCC, pp. 61-62.

[4] *Ibid.,* 30. LCC V, p. 342. Jerome, *Dialogue Against the Luciferians,* 19. NPNF VI, p. 329.

[5] Theodoret, *Church History,* V.1. LCC III, p. 344.

[6] *Decree of Chalcedon.* LCC III, p. 372.

[7] Gregory of Nazianzus, *Epistle 202.* LCC III, p. 231.

[8] *Ibid., Epistle 201.* LCC III, p. 216.

[9] Theodoret, *Church History,* V.10-13. LCC III, p. 344.

[10] Quoted in *Acts of the Council of Ephesus.* LCC III, pp. 347-48.

[11] Cyril, *Second Letter to Nestorius.* DCC, p. 68.

[12] Cyril, *Third Letter to Nestorius.* LCC III, pp. 353-54.

[13] Formula of Union of 433. LCC III, p. 356.

[14] *Council of Constantinople,* Session vii. DCC, p. 69.

[15] *Tome of Leo,* 3, 4. LCC III, pp. 363-65.

[16] *The Chalcedonian Decree.* LCC III, p. 373.

[17] See above, p. (96).

[18] John 15:26.

[19] Augustine, *On Free Will,* III.xxi.60; *On the Trinity,* IX.18, X.18, XV.48. LCC VI, p. 207; VIII, pp. 77, 88, 177.

[20] Augustine, *The City of God,* X.24, XI.24. Translation by Marcus Dods (Edinburgh, 1871) I, pp. 414, 465.

[21] Augustine, *Confessions,* XIII.ix.10; XIII.xi.12; XIII.xxii.32. LCC VII, pp. 304, 306, 319.

[22] This is reproduced from an 1863 edition of the English *Book of Common Prayer.* Note the colon dividing each verse, to facilitate the singing of the *Quicunque vult* to Anglican chant settings.

[23] Augustine, *On the Trinity,* XV.49, 50, 51. LCC VIII, pp. 179, 181.

IX. In Essentia Unitas

[1] Translation by the Reverend F. X. Lasance in *The New Missal for Every Day* (New York, 1915) pp. 104-05.

[2] *Book of Common Prayer* (1928) p. 79. (All printings of this prayerbook have the same pagination.)

[3] See above, pp. 85-86.

[4] See above, p. 102.

[5] Claudius of Turin, *Defense and Reply to Theodemir.* LCC IX, p. 247.

[6] Rupert of Deutz, *Commentary on Saint John.* LCC IX, pp. 262-63.

[7] St. Anselm, Cur Deus Homo, XVIII. LCC X, p. 179.

[8] Richard of St. Victor, *On the Trinity,* III.ii. LCC X, pp. 331-32.

[9] Peter Abelard, *Hymn for Saturday Vespers.* Translation by John Mason Neale, 1854. No. 596 in the *Service Book and Hymnal of the Lutheran Church in America* (Philadelphia, 1958); No. 589 in *The Hymnal of the Protestant Episcopal Church in the United States of America* (New York, 1940).

[10] John Hus, *On Simony,* 2. LCC XIV, p. 201.

[11] Augsburg Confession, Article I. In Christian Heinrich Schott, *The Unaltered Augsburg Confession* (New York, 1850) p. 4.

[12] Martin Luther, Epistle Sermon for Trinity Sunday. In Hugh Thompson Kerr, editor, *A Compend of Luther's Theology* (Philadelphia, 1943) pp. 41f.

[13] Cf. Origen, *On Prayer,* XV.1-4. Anselm, *Cur Deus Homo,* IX. LCC II, pp. 269-271; vol. X, pp. 154-55.

[14] John Calvin, *Institutes of the Christian Religion,* I.xiii,2-4. LCC XX, pp. 123-125.

[15] Westminster Confession of Faith, II.iii. Quoted in Archibald Alexander Hodge, *A Commentary on the Confession of Faith* (Philadelphia, 1869) p. 83.

[16] Albert Peel, editor, *The Savoy Declaration of Faith and Order, 1658* (London, 1939) p. 47.

[17] Articles of Religion I, II, V.

[18] *The Racovian Catechism,* III.i. Edited and translated by Thomas Rees (London, 1818) pp. 34, 37, 39.

[19] See George Newton Conklin, *Biblical Criticism and Heresy in Milton* (New York, 1949) pp. 37-38, 97-98.

[20] Quoted in Maurice Kelley, *This Great Argument: a Study of Milton's* De Doctrina Christiana *as a Gloss upon* Paradise Lost (Gloucester, Massachusetts, 1962) pp. 86-87.

[21] I Timothy 1:17.

[22] Georg Wilhelm Friedrich Hegel, *Lectures on the Philosophy of Religion* (transl. E. B. Speirs and J. Burdon Sanderson, London, 1895) Vol. III, pp. 99-100. See also *ibid.*, pp. 9-33.

[23] George A. Gordon, *Ultimate Conceptions of Faith* (Boston, 1903) pp. 357, 371-72.

[24] J. R. Illingworth, *The Doctrine of the Trinity Apologetically Considered* (London, 1907) pp. 243, 240, 252.

[25] See Leonard Hodgson, *The Doctrine of the Trinity* (London, 1943) pp. 68, 85-112.

Continuance: THE REALITIES

[1] John 1:43-49; Matthew 27:54 = Mark 15:39; John 1:14.

[2] See above, p. 92.

[3] The Disciples of Christ still hold to Alexander Campbell's non-Trinitarian position. In Hymn No. 107 of *Christian Worship: A Hymnal* (St. Louis, 1941) issued jointly with the Northern (now American) Baptist Convention, the last lines of the first and fourth stanzas of Bishop Reginald Heber's classic hymn for Trinity Sunday, "Holy, Holy, Holy," have been changed from "God in three Persons, blessed Trinity," to "God over all, and blest eternally." The Baptist edition has kept the original phrasing. For Dr. Richardson's view see especially "A Christological Note" in his *The Doctrine of the Trinity* (New York, 1958) pp. 150-152.

[4] Henry P. Van Dusen, *Spirit, Son and Father* (New York, 1958) pp. 173-74. Walter Russell Bowie, *Jesus and the Trinity* (New York, 1960) pp. 143-44.

[5] I John 3:24.

[6] This is the phrasing in the American *Book of Common Prayer,* taken from Cranmer's first Prayer Book of 1549. The Latin of the Roman Mass is magnificent: *Per ipsum, et cum ipso,*

et in ipso, est tibi Deo Patri omnipotenti, in unitate Spiritus Sancti, omnis honor et gloria. Per omnia saecula saeculorum: but the English translations authorized by Rome limp badly.

Index

INDEX

Abelard, Peter, 105, 140

Adoptionism, 29f, 40

Alexander, Bishop of Alexandria, 78f

Altizer, Thomas J. J., 56, 131, 137

Angels, 11-13, 20f, 44

Anselm, 105, 107, 140

Apollinaris, Apollinarianism, 90f, 115, 122f

Apostles' Creed, x, 36, 70

Aquinas, Thomas, 105f

Aristotle, 23, 105f

Arius, Arianism, 78-87, 95, 108, 138

Articles of Religion, 108f, 140

Aruminum, 86f

Athanasian Creed, 98-102, 108, 139

Athanasius, 80f, 83-87, 108, 139

Athenagoras, 39, 47, 60f, 71f, 135-38

Augsburg Confession, 106f, 140

Augustine, 96-98, 101f, 104f, 139

Baptism, 45, 68-70, 73

Basil the Great, 87

Biddle, John, 111

"Blasphemy of Sirmium," 85f, 104

Bowie, Walter Russell, 125, 141

Calvin, John, 107-09, 140

Campbell, Alexander, 65, 124, 141

Chalcedon, Council of, 88f, 93-95, 102, 108, 123f, 139

Channing, William Ellery, 114

Charlemagne, 95

Chillingworth, William, 111

Christos, 33f

Church of England, 97, 101, 103, 108f

Claudius of Turin, 105, 140

Clement of Alexandria, 23, 39, 135

"Comforter," 46f

Constantine I, 79, 81, 84

Constantinople, Council of, 87f, 90f, 95, 108

Constantius II, 84f

145

Cranmer, Thomas, 89, 141
Cromwell, Oliver, 111
Cyprian, 73, 138
Cyril of Alexandria, 91f, 94, 139

Dead Sea scrolls, 18f, 134
"Death of God" theology, ix, 56, 120, 131
Didache, 69f, 138
Diognetus, Letter to, 39, 60, 135, 137

Ebionites, 30
Epicharmus, 24, 134
Epiphanius, 74f, 135, 138
Erasmus, 64, 106
Eusebius of Caesarea, 48, 79-82, 95, 136, 139
Eusebius of Nicomedia, 78, 138
Eutyches, 93

Filioque, 18, 89, 94-97, 109, 126
Fosdick, Harry Emerson, 125
Franklin, Benjamin, 114

Gehenna, 51f
Gilder, Richard Watson, 122
Gloria Patri, v, 114
Glossolalia, 43f
Gnosticism, 58, 79, 82

Goodspeed, Edgar J., 65
Gordon, George A., 116, 141
Gregory I, Pope, 103
Gregory of Nazianzus, 90, 139

Hamilton, William, 131
Harnack, Adolf, 58, 137
Hegel, Georg Wilhelm Friedrich, 115f, 141
Heraclides, Dialogue with, 39f, 135, 138
Heraclitus, 23f, 38, 134f
Hilary of Poitiers, 86f
Hinduism, 57f
Hippolytus, 23, 48, 136
Hocking, William Ernest, 134
Hodgkin, Wilfred R. H., 119
Hodgson, Leonard, 117f, 141
Homoousios, Homoiousios, 81, 85f, 108
Honest to God, ix, 131
Hosius of Cordova, 79-81, 84
Hus, John, 106, 140
Hypostasis, 75-77, 87, 107, 125

Illingworth, J. R., 116f, 141
Irenaeus, 58f, 61, 70, 134, 137f

James I, King, 108, 111
"Jehovah," 2f

Jerome, 64, 76, 87, 138f
JHVH, 1-11, 61
John XXII, Pope, 103
Justin Martyr, 35f, 39, 59, 70, 134, 136-38

Kenosis, 28, 37, 39f, 56

Latitudinarians, 111, 113
Leo I, Pope, 93f, 139
Leo III, Pope, 95
Leo XIII, Pope, 65
Logos, 16-18, 23-25, 28, 37-40, 58, 90, 123
Luther, Martin, 107, 140
Lutheranism, 98, 103, 106-08

Marcion, Marcionism, 58-60
Marcus Aurelius Antoninus, 24f, 39, 134
McGiffert, Arthur Cushman, 27, 134
Messiah, Messianism, 28, 30-34, 58, 123
Milton, John, 112f, 141
Modalism, *see* Sabellianism
Moffatt, James, 20f, 65
Monophysitism, 91-94
Montanus, Montanism, 48f, 72f

Nestorius, Nestorianism, 91f

Nicea, Council of, 63, 72, 79-83, 108
Nicene Creed, x, 80-83, 85, 88f, 108
Nicholas I, Pope, 95f

Old Roman Symbol, 36
Origen, 39f, 49, 77f, 107, 135f, 138, 140
Ousia, 76, 85-87, 125

Parakletos, 47
Patripassianism, 74, 90, 126
Pelagius II, Pope, 103f
Pentecost, 14f, 29, 43f
Per ipsum, 127, 141f
Persona, 73f, 107, 126
Philo Judaeus, 16-18, 25, 37f, 134f
Pike, James A., ix, 131
Plato, Platonism, 105f
Polycarp, 58
Priestley, Joseph, 113
Priscillian, 65

Quicunque vult, 98-102, 108, 139

Racovian Catechism, 110-12, 140
Regula fidei, 70

Richard of St. Victor, 105, 140

Richardson, Cyril C., ix, 124, 131

Robinson, John A. T., ix, 131

Roosevelt, Theodore, 125

Ruach, 12f, 16

Rupert of Deutz, 105, 140

Sabellius, Sabellianism, 74f, 78f, 84f, 97, 108, 125f

Savoy Declaration of Faith and Order, 108, 140

Servetus, Michael, 109

Shema Yisrael, 1f

Sirmium, 85f, 104

Socinianism, 110-13, 115

Socinus, Faustus, 109f

"Son(s) of God," 20-23, 33-37, 123

Spencer, Francis Aloysius, 65, 137f

Stoicism, Stoics, 24, 37-39

Substantia, 75f, 85f, 104

Tertullian, 48f, 72-75, 77, 134, 136, 138

Theotokos, 91-94

Tongues, Gift of, 43f

Trinitas, 72-74, 107f

Ulfilas, 87

Unitarianism, Unitarians, 110-15, 126

Vahanian, Gabriel, 131

Van Buren, Paul, 131

Van Dusen, Henry P., 125, 141

Virgin Birth, 34-36

Wesley, John, 109

Westminster Confession, 108, 140

"Wisdom," 16-18

Wycliffe, John, 106

Type, 11 on 13 and 10 on 11 Garamond
Display, Garamond
Paper, White Standard "R" Antique